"What I know about Robert Rogers is that he adores God and cherishes his family. On one horrific day, he lost everything most precious on this planet – his wife and all four children. And without hope in Christ, Robert's own journey most certainly would have ended very differently to where he stands today.

I encourage you to read this book and be inspired and reminded about the reality of what living IN CHRIST can truly look like. Much love, Darlene Zschech."

⬧ Darlene Zschech, Singer, songwriter (*"Shout to the Lord"*), worship leader, author, speaker, and co-pastor of *Hope Unlimited Church*, New South Wales, Australia.

"At the end of your life you want to look back and have no regrets! To do this you need to start living today with your end in mind.

Robert Rogers gives you the tools to live your life in such a way that when it is all over you will have lived a life that made a difference. Robert gives us 7 great and practical steps that will let you live a life with no regrets.

Read this book and start the process!"

⬧ Father Larry Richards, Pastor of *Saint Joseph Church*, Erie, Pennsylvania, and author of *Be a Man! Becoming the Man God Created You to Be* and *Surrender! The Life-Changing Power of Doing God's Will.*

"Robert, I absolutely LOVED reading your new book, *7 Steps to No Regrets!* It should be read by everyone! What an inspired and heartfelt heart-wrenching, soul-searching, reality-checking, and masterful Scripture study all rolled into 182 pages!! All of Heaven must be shouting, *'Well done, good and faithful servant!'* God is using you mightily! I think this book should be mandatory reading for all engaged and married couples!"

Barbara McGuigan, EWTN TV and Radio Host of *Open Line* and *The Good Fight.*

"By the grace of God, Robert Rogers has turned the unspeakable tragedy of losing his wife and four children into a lesson for us all: live every moment of life with no regrets. Following his *7 Steps to No Regrets* can provide us the happiness we seek in this world, and ultimately a place at the Lord's Table in Heaven."

William Croyle, Author of *Finding Peace Amid the Chaos, Angel in the Rubble,* & *I Choose to be Happy.*

Also by Robert Rogers:

Into the Deep: one man's story of how tragedy took his family but could not take his faith (Tyndale, 2007)

"His children will be mighty in the land." Psalm 112

Mighty in the Land Ministry
Fort Wayne, Indiana

7 Steps to No Regrets

How to find peace of mind with God, others, and yourself

Robert Rogers

Mighty in the Land Ministry
Fort Wayne, Indiana

Edited by Rosemary Henderson
Cover design by Eddy Mora, *IdentityBox, Inc.*, Olathe, KS.
Back cover family photo by Robert Rogers. Author photo by Inga Rogers.
ISBN-13: 978-0-9793953-9-0
Printed in the United States of America
First edition: September 2013

Dedicated to my father,

George H. Rogers (1929 - 2012)

…the strongest, wisest, most courageous, compassionate, kindhearted, selfless, gentle, patient and loving man I've ever known.

Throughout 60 years of marriage to my mother and 83 years of life, he exemplified a life of no regrets unto his final breath.

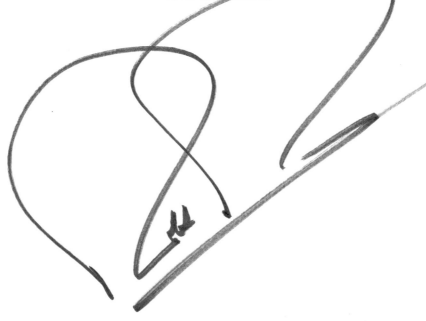

*"I am leaving you with a gift -- peace of mind and heart.
And the peace I give isn't like the peace the world gives.
So don't be troubled or afraid."*

-Jesus

(John 14:27)

Contents

Prologue

Are You Ready?

"…my beautiful wife, Melissa, was found yesterday morning. She did not survive the tragedy."

With my head still spinning, my heart still hemorrhaging, my eyes still gushing, my soul still reeling, and my faith still sustaining, somehow I poured forth these words at 1:51 A.M. on that somberly stagnant morning: Wednesday, September 3rd, 2003.

I sat uprightly and yet awkwardly on the empty bed of my daughter, Makenah, typing on my laptop in her dimly lit room, illuminated only by the computer screen's stark glare and the dainty lamp on her nightstand. She had wrapped the lamp base with tissue paper and written the words "God Loves Me" across it. Yes, indeed, my precious daughter.

Just a few days earlier, my life had tragically, dramatically, and completely changed forever. Now, in just a few hours, I was scheduled to give a press conference in my home community of Liberty, Missouri, to bring the greater Kansas City metropolitan area up to date on the tragedy which befell my family over Labor

Day weekend. I continued pouring my heart through my tears and onto the keys of the computer as I pondered our past 12 years.

"Melissa and I were blessed with a 'fairytale' courtship and marriage…We courted in New England…married on New Year's Eve…and moved to California…We seized many moments in time and passionately enjoyed life together. I have no regrets."

No regrets. Yes, it truly was a life of no regrets. Not perfect by any means. Yet, looking back, we got the most important things right – with God and with our family. Thank God. No regrets whatsoever.

God knows I messed up plenty, stuck my foot in my mouth, and spent a few nights "in the dog house" as a husband. I struggled to sacrificially love my wife the same way Christ loves the Church – giving up His very life. His mandate in Scripture to me as a husband remained my daily challenge and example to follow.

"And you husbands must love your wives with the same love Christ showed the church. He gave up his life for her…" (Ephesians 5:25)

I had done my best throughout our years to let go of myself and my wishes, and to love Melissa sacrificially – giving myself up for her. I have an entire shoebox stuffed with scraps of paper – brimming full of love notes between us. My heart is chocked full and overflowing with memories from our romantic getaways, dates…and ice cream.

I typed some more.

"… Ice cream made for sweet bookends to a sweet and rich marriage…"

As my mind raced and ricocheted through sweet memories, I reminisced on the life with which Melissa and I were blessed – from our first date at an ice cream parlor in Boston 13 years ago – to our final family feast at an ice cream shop in Wichita, only moments before the cataclysmic catastrophe Saturday night.

Saturday night.

It hit me all over as I melted into a puddle of tears again – right there on Makenah's bed. I couldn't stop replaying it over and over in my mind. Now, it seemed like an eternity away, even though it was barely over three days ago.

Saturday evening, August 30th, 2003, was when my worst nightmare slammed me in the face. It was every parent's worst nightmare. But now, this was more than just a bad dream…it was my reality.

Melissa, our four children – Makenah (8), Zachary (5), Nicholas (3), Alenah (1) – and I were just returning from a relative's wedding in Wichita, Kansas. After the reception, we splurged on ice cream with some relatives. We laughed and talked while our children played with one another.

Around 8:00 P.M. we began our three hour trip home, stopping first at a gas station, where we found temporary but welcome relief from the incessantly pounding rain. About an hour into the dark drive to Kansas City, with Melissa at the wheel for the first leg of our ride back, we pummeled into a flash flood – the kind that apparently comes only once every hundred years to this part of Kansas. It was all utterly unfathomable.

A summer drought had prompted myriad prayers for rain. Now, a stalled storm system remnant from Hurricane Isabella soaked the parched Flint Hills of Kansas all weekend, dumping nearly nine inches of rain in just the past few hours. Finally, everyone's prayers were answered – everyone's but ours – so it appeared.

Our lifetime of trusting God through multiple trials and step-stones of faith had compelled us just that morning to recite my father's safe-driving prayer during our journey to the Wichita wedding.

"Dear Lord, if it be Your holy will, please grant that we would have a safe journey – with no mishaps whatsoever, involving us and other people, our vehicles and the vehicles of others, our property and the property of others. We ask this, dear Jesus, in Your Holy Name so that we and others may always and better serve, in Your Holy Name, to Your greater honor and glory. Not our will, but Yours be done. In the name of the Father, and of the Son, and of the Holy Spirit, Amen."

As the youngest of eight children raised in an actively rich Catholic Christian tradition, my parents composed that marvelous prayer decades ago. Growing up, we recited it every time we crammed all ten of us into our VW Bus for a campout or vacation. Through that simple prayer, God had truly protected all of our extended families for numerous years and countless thousands of miles.

Now, after nearly 12 years of marriage, three challenging childbirths, two C-sections, two miscarriages (one nearly fatal), our autistic son with Down syndrome (Zachary), and our special-needs daughter adopted from China (Alenah), Melissa and I had learned to trust God and cherish our family to the fullest.

After God, our children came first. They were the most precious portion of our lives. We loved them to pieces and couldn't get enough of them. We did our best to make memories with them every day. We also prayed fervently over them for God's protection from all harm. We endeavored to live a life of no regrets – as best we could.

But this night, the ride home was beyond treacherous. Pitch black. Torrential rain. Windshield wipers swiping full-blast. Melissa – a marvelous driver with an impeccable record – followed other taillights on the Kansas Turnpike and avoided hydroplaning as the pouring rain pounded the pavement.

We suddenly splashed into an enormous river flowing right-to-left across the interstate. The water was instantly up to our headlights, lapping against the bumper. Within mere minutes it overwhelmed our minivan, seeped into the floorboards, rose to the seat cushions, then up to the steering wheel, and quickly stalled the engine.

The chaos and chilling water awoke our sleeping children from their weary slumber. One by one, realizing the inescapable terror overtaking us, they soon began crying uncontrollably. The forceful rapids pinned our vehicle against the concrete median – trapped by a raging river now over four feet deep and nearly a thousand feet wide – inundating us at 32,000 gallons every second.

With no feasible way to rescue our family on foot, we huddled in our minivan and beseeched unto God, "Jesus, save us…Jesus, save us!"

We quoted Psalm 46 crying aloud, *"God is our refuge and strength, an ever-present help in trouble. Therefore we will not fear, though the earth give way…though its waters roar and foam…"* (Psalm 46:1-3 NIV)

We sang a song of praise, "*Lord, I Lift Your Name on High…*" trying to calm our children with familiar music.

Scripture, praise, and the name of Jesus: these were the three crucial elements our lips uttered at the most perilous moment of our lives.

My mind raced and wrestled with what to do. As a husband and father, it was my responsibility to protect and provide for my family. As a rational engineer of thirteen years, the magnitude and scope of this sudden situation baffled my brain and befuddled every fathomable fiber of my being. Now, I felt grossly inadequate and completely out of control. It was utterly incomprehensible.

Every inch the water rose I thought *it can't possibly get any worse.*

Only, it did.

Less than 20 minutes after we first collided with the water, everything broke loose.

At 9:18 P.M. eyewitnesses described a *"wall of water"* seven feet high and 200 feet wide crashing across the freeway, consuming everything in its path – including vehicles and over 100,000 pounds of concrete median. We were thrust into the deluge…plunged into the deep.

As the raging rapids washed our minivan along the torrent, with our children still screaming, I instinctively kicked out the window as a last-ditch effort to rescue our family. As the window burst, the overwhelming pressure from the water outside – compressed against the air bubble inside – was similar to popping a balloon. The surge of water flushed everything and everyone out that wasn't tied down. Melissa, Makenah, and I were all out of our seatbelts and now consumed by water.

Instantly I was sucked out and submerged in the torrent, tumbling as a rag doll in a washing machine, out of control and completely at the mercy of the current...and of God. Strangely, I sensed an indescribable peace as I was drowning, as if all six of us were ascending to Heaven.

Astonishing as it may seem, God was there. Amidst the chaos and confusion, God's peace was near.

He wasn't absent. He was present.

Though it defied explanation, He still hadn't left us, just as the Scripture we recited in the van moments ago promised.

"...though its waters roar and foam and the mountains quake with their surging...the Lord Almighty is with us..." (Psalm 46:3, 7 NIV)

Somehow, my head surfaced and bobbed above the water as I coughed and gasped for air, grasping for tree branches and anything to hold onto. It was utterly futile. Completely disoriented, the flash flood swept me downstream at insurmountable speed. Though I'm a good swimmer, there's no way I could overcome the force of this flash flood. No way...humanly speaking.

But somehow, God intervened. I felt earth beneath my knees as I was washed ashore on the left bank. I crawled out onto the slippery mud, raised my hands against the hammering rain, and cried out to God repeatedly, "Oh God, oh God!" as the droplets collided with tears on my face. Over and over, I wailed loudly and searched frantically for my family. I couldn't see or hear a thing beyond the deafening, relentless tempest.

In frigid, traumatic shock and depleted strength, I made my way as best I could over a half mile back to the freeway for help – scaling a barbed-wire fence and crawling up the embankment. Stumbling at the top onto the pavement, I cried out to the first officer on the scene, "My wife and four children are still down there!" They immediately began a search-and-rescue for my family as they ushered me to an ambulance.

After three excruciatingly long hours later, with no other apparent signs of life, my hemorrhaging heart grew heavier by the minute. The treacherous floodwaters gradually subsided. They transported me to a nearby hospital to tend to my wounds. They treated and discharged me in miraculously fair condition, allowing me to remain in a starkly empty room in an unused hospital wing.

Around 5:00 A.M., still shivering in chilling shock on the bed under several white hospital blankets, an officer and chaplain approached me in my dimly-lit room. With their hats on their chests, I hoped for the best – but feared the worst. With much trepidation, I slipped out from under the covers, braced my feet on the floor, and faced those words that every parent prays are never uttered in their presence…or in their lifetime.

"Mr. Rogers, we need to ask you to identify the bodies of your three youngest children. They are dead."

Stunned.

Shell-shocked.

They had found our minivan upside-down, a mile and a half from the freeway. Zachary, Nicholas, and Alenah were still strapped in their car seats.

No words adequately describe my excruciating emotions at that moment. But, I had to face it – as if God just grabbed hold of the hair on the back of my head, shoved my face in it, and in essence said, "Go ahead, Robert. Face it. My grace really is *that* sufficient."

"My grace is sufficient for you, for My strength is made perfect in weakness." (2 Corinthians 12:9 NKJV)

Still in a surreal daze, the officer led me out of the room and down a never-ending hallway – the kind that seems to get longer and longer the more steps you take. They pulled back the drape which, up to now, still cloaked the emergency room.

What I saw made every ounce of blood go to my toes. As the veil lifted, I beheld my children – Zachary, Nicholas, and Alenah – now cold, wet, and lifeless.

Aghast at the dreadful sight, I immediately collapsed over each of their bodies and wailed incessantly, crying out to God as I identified them, one by one.

I didn't want to leave them. And yet, I knew they had already left me. I knew they were already in the presence of the Almighty.

I reluctantly let go. I agonizingly surrendered them back to God. "Father, into Your Hands I commend their spirits." They were His all along. They weren't mine to keep forever.

Several hours later, they found Makenah caught on a barbed-wire fence along the path of the flash flood near our minivan. I had to muster up the strength to tread down that long hallway again and somehow identify Daddy's first little girl. My stomach ached from my incessant tears.

Finally, after three excruciating days in the Emporia hospital, holding out hope with my parents and relatives now at my side, they finally found Melissa – the love of my life. Her body was two miles from the freeway in a retention pond that had tripled in size from the flood waters. Alongside my parents and siblings, I identified her lifeless remains as well – my bride of nearly 12 years.

Each of my precious family members – once brimming and overflowing with life – was suddenly, starkly still. I groaned from my gut as never before, reeling and feeling as if I was going to vomit each time I cried. As my heart bled, more and more of me spilled out.

I gathered up the remnants of my courage and determined to somehow grip the pain and face it head on. I wasn't about to give up, but I felt as though my faith was about to give in.

I wrestled with how our loving God could allow this to happen to our family. We trusted Him through Zachary's Down syndrome ordeals, through Alenah's special-needs adoption just eight months ago, and countless other trials. He brought us this far through so much...all for this? As the sole-survivor, I had a lot of tough questions for God.

Was this some kind of cruel joke? Why didn't I die that night and accompany my family to Heaven? Why?... Why me?... Why not me?

My tough questions were met with stark silence.

"...Moses entered into the deep darkness where God was." (Exodus 20:21)

Sometimes in the deepest darkness, we tap into God's deepest grace. In the still silence, we discover God's still small voice.

God was there.

"Do not be afraid...I have called you by name; you are mine. When you go through deep waters and great trouble, I will be with you. When you go through rivers of difficulty, you will not drown! ...For I am the Lord...your Savior." (Isaiah 43:1-3)

Scripture – His very Words – whispered life. It spoke volumes to me when I needed it most. It was beckoning me...challenging me to trust God more deeply, even when it hurt...even when it didn't make any sense.

After three of the worst days of my life, we left Emporia, Kansas, for our home in Liberty, Missouri. The two-hour drive seemed to last forever as the blazing sun descended in the rear-view mirror, coloring the Kansas sky. I didn't want to enter the night...the darkness...nor my empty, hollow home that still echoed of my family's voices.

One step at a time and with the strength of God alone, I faced the darkness, the memories, the pictures, the toys, the empty beds, the stagnant swing set, the dirty dishes, the laundry, the artwork on the refrigerator – each of them – one item at a time.

The local police requested a press conference for Wednesday afternoon – the day after they found Melissa. I couldn't sleep. After getting up around 1:00 in the morning and preparing my comments, I finished typing at 6:47 A.M. Following a tearful and awkward breakfast with my parents and siblings, several police cars escorted us to the press conference location.

I stood uprightly and lifted my head in front of a dizzying array of cameras and microphones. As I choked up and bridled back my tears, I somehow made it through my written statements, swallowing my pain all along the way.

> *"...I know that there is a God and that He loves us – and he wants us to live with Him... When God is our refuge, even when there is despair – there is hope! Even in the midst of sorrow – there is peace and joy!*
>
> *...in my weakness – God is strong. This tragedy may have shattered my family, but it will not shatter my resolve to hope for good. ...God came that we might have life - more abundantly.*
>
> *To honor the memory of my wife and children with something positive out of this terrible tragedy, please love, cherish, and savor your families every day. Hug and play with them. Eat meals and pray together, and tell your family you love them every day.*
>
> *I'm not bitter against God. I've had a full, abundant life and I'm fully persuaded that somehow, by His grace, he will turn this tragedy into good. He has graced me with a blessed, abundant life. Now, he has given my wife and children a blessed and abundant life everlasting.*

>*...We seized many moments in time and passionately enjoyed life together.*
>*I have no regrets."*

No regrets, indeed.

People who tuned in to the live press conference were evidently stunned by my words of hope amidst such overwhelming devastation. Requests inundated television stations to re-air the broadcast in its entirety.

The words that poured out of my mouth were simply words from Scripture that we had poured into our hearts for years as a family. From memorizing multiple verses, these Words of Life were ingrained into the fabric of my soul.

I found that when life squeezes you, whatever is in your heart will gush out of your mouth – similar to squeezing a tube of toothpaste.

So, how about you?

What is in your heart?

Many years have now passed since the flood. I can still say, "I have no regrets."

Can you?

Can you honestly say, "I have no regrets"?

Are you at peace?

Or are you living with regrets? Do you feel trapped – harboring the past?

If so, I'd like to do my best to open my heart with you now to share how I came to live this life of no regrets.

We serve a God of second chances. He has just given you another chance to make things right – right now. Yesterday is gone. None of us is guaranteed the next five seconds. So, don't wait another moment. Please keep reading. Don't wait for another tragedy, natural disaster, or funeral to change your priorities and make things right.

Today counts.

You may never get another opportunity such as this. Life is extremely fragile and can change in a moment.

I know.

If your world is suddenly washed away or turned upside-down tomorrow, I earnestly want you to truly be able to say from your heart, "I have no regrets."

So, are you ready?

If you are willing, then come journey with me through these simple *7 Steps to No Regrets*. Please heed these words and take them to heart. It has literally cost me everything to share them with you. I pray they take root and dramatically transform your life.

Step 1
Chapter One

The Ultimate Regret

> *"This is what the Lord says: 'Let not the wise man gloat in his wisdom, or the mighty man in his might, or the rich man in his riches. Let them boast in this alone: that they truly know me…'"* (Jeremiah 9:23-24)

"One thing," declared Curly in the movie, *City Slickers*, smiling as he held up his ragged and jagged finger amidst the arid Western air.

"Your finger?" responded Billy Crystal's character, Mitch, in disbelief. He wanted desperately to know the secret of life – that "One Thing" – from this rugged old, crusty cowboy.

Curly never answered what that "One Thing" was, except that Mitch had to figure it out for himself.

I'm convinced this one thing in life is the root, the basis, and the secret of living a life of no regrets.

Without it, we miss the peace that calms our soul through any storm – or flash flood. With it, we have the peaceful assurance and undergirding to guide our ship through life's treacherous waters and ultimately into a tranquil beautiful expanse. If we miss that "One Thing", then we'll experience the worst regret of our lives.

So, what is the worst regret in life…ever?

Perhaps something you did or didn't do? Perhaps that nagging grudge or unrelenting unforgiveness you're avoiding? Perhaps too few times saying, "I love you"?

In the years following the death of my family, I'm grateful that I still have no regrets with my personal actions and behavior. Thankfully I never delved into any drugs, drunkenness, or promiscuity. Rather, I immersed myself into Scripture – God's very Word – because I knew that nothing else would satisfy. I realized something would consume me, and I wanted it to be God alone.

Even amidst the vast void of tender love and affection of my dearly departed family – no more embracing hugs, no more sweet "I love you" whispered into my ears – I discovered something that truly blew my mind.

I found that God really was enough. His grace actually was sufficient.

God's Words in the Bible were literally life and health to me. Day by day and tear by tear, they gradually restored my soul.

I didn't idly sit around or mope in a ball of self-pity and misery. I grieved and cried continually – as wave after wave slammed me and melted me into a puddle again. But I grieved *with hope* because of my faith in Christ.

My faith didn't remove the pain, but it got me through the pain. Trusting God didn't diminish or vanquish the anguish, but it enabled me to endure it. I never held back any tears because each one seemed to help wash away another speck of insurmountable grief, bit by bit.

For three solid years, I underwent professional grief counseling. I highly recommend that to anyone who has lost a loved one. I also ate lots of ice cream and peanut butter. I highly recommend that, too. Chocolate therapy is a very happy place for me. If today were my last day, I might regret that I haven't yet sampled every possible flavor of ice cream.

Regrets can exist all around us. However, one supreme regret surpasses them all.

How about eternal life? That is forever.

Each of us will live forever…somewhere.

Eternity may seem unsettling and uncomfortable because many of us just aren't sure what's going to happen when we die. I discovered from the flash flood that death can creep up on us at any time, without warning.

Life is incredibly fragile.

So, here it is: I believe the worst regret in life is to miss the ultimate goal – our eternal home – Heaven. If we blow it on this single issue, nothing else matters. If we miss this mark, we've missed it all.

At the end of our lives, the only thing that will truly matter is relationships – starting with God. Our relationship with God determines our eternal trajectory.

The worst regret in life is eternal regret.

For all other regrets, you now have a second chance to amend them. However, there is one choice in life that you might never get another chance to change. The only opportunity you have to make that decision is right now. Yesterday is past, and tomorrow may never come.

"God put us in the world to know, to love, and to serve Him, and so to come to paradise." (CCC 1721)

This is the meaning of life – the whole reason we exist. It's a truth I learned as a youngster. Back then I never realized the depth of its profound simplicity. Making it to Heaven – to paradise – hinges on knowing God.

Imagine if today was your last day and God Almighty asked, "Why should I let you into Heaven?" Perhaps some might respond, "Well, I tried to be a good person. I helped a lot of people and went to church." All of those things are great. Now, imagine if God responded, "Get out of here; I never *knew* you. You never took the time to *know* Me." In Holy Scripture, Jesus predicted this will actually happen.

"Not everyone who says to Me, 'Lord, Lord' shall enter the kingdom of heaven, but he who does the will of My Father in heaven...I will declare to them, 'I never knew you; depart from Me...'" (Matthew 7:21, 23 NKJV)

Jesus just described life's worst regret. Evidently, religious people who paid Him lip service, called to Him "Lord, Lord" and even performed signs in His name blew it. They missed the single most important thing in life – and ended up paying for it – forever.

It appears they did not *know* Jesus in a personal way. They *called* Him "Lord" but apparently never *made* Him their Lord. They could name Him, but didn't know Him. It was only skin-deep. Privately, it never involved their heart. God wasn't their way of life.

I've been guilty of this. How about you?

"I know all the things you do, that you are neither hot nor cold. I wish you were one or the other! But since you are like lukewarm water, I will spit you out of my mouth!" (Revelation 3:15-16)

Early in life, I was comfortably warm on the outside – just enough to fool everyone else – but cold on the inside. As a whole, I was barely lukewarm.

God wants me hot or cold – not somewhere wishy-washy in-between. He desires us to have a passionate fire burning for Him – just as He does for us, *"...for he is a God who is passionate about his relationship with you."* (Exodus 34:14)

Are you passionate about your relationship with Him? For a long while, I wasn't. My comfortable church membership kept me from delving into a deeper divine relationship.

It's one thing to be religious and slap on a Sunday morning sticker.

What does God call you? What is your relationship with Him? Does He call you His own – one of His sheep? Does He call you a follower of Christ? Jesus said, *"My sheep listen to my voice; I know them, and they follow me. I give them eternal life…"* (John 10:27-28 GNT)

It's so easy to slip into the rut of religion – merely following rules, obligations, and traditions – and miss following Christ entirely. Too often, we substitute "God-made" with "man-made" and let religion take God's place.

In another parable, Jesus articulated the worst regret in life again. Five foolish women and five wise ones each had lamps that appeared good from the outside. Some had plenty of oil to stay lit for the Bridegroom's wedding. Others were empty inside and vacant when the time came.

Sometimes we are that way. We put on a good show and look good from the outside. Inside however, our hearts are bare and hollow.

As they heard the Bridegroom coming, the foolish ones begged to borrow oil from the wise ones at the last moment to fill their vessels. However, this is something you must possess personally on your own – not beg or borrow. You can't even rely on the faith of your fathers or family – nor on your legacy or traditions – however enriching and marvelous they might be. There are no spiritual grandchildren. It must come from deep within your own personal vessel. It must come from your heart.

Feverishly, the desperate ones quickly ran out to buy some oil at the last minute. Try to imagine their horror as they returned…only to find the door shut and bolted.

They missed it…forever.

Eternal regrets.

Mortified, they shouted, *"'Lord, Lord, open to us!'"* Ironically, they *called* Him "Lord." Tragically, they evidently never *made* Him or *knew* Him *as* Lord. For *"…he answered and said, 'Assuredly, I say to you, I do not know you.'"* (Matthew 25:12 NKJV) *"For many…will seek to enter and will not be able. When once the Master of the house has risen up and shut the door, and you begin to stand outside and knock at the door, saying, 'Lord, Lord, open for us,' and He will answer and say to you, 'I do not know you…'"* (Luke 13:24-25 NKJV)

How I wish this were merely a sad story. This parable is a prophetic prediction of what will happen to many people because, *"narrow is the gate…which leads to life, and there are few who find it."* (Matthew 7:14 NKJV)

I hope the raw reality of these verses stops you in your tracks as they did me as a teenager. They should. These Scriptures should slam the reality of the worst regret smack dab in the middle of our foreheads with a baseball bat.

I was one of those who had a lamp that looked good from the outside. I was a good person. I went to church regularly. I was an altar server. I lived by the rules and did everything I was obliged to do. I could play a convincing game and talk a good talk.

My faith wasn't alive. I didn't walk what I talked. I didn't have peace with God.

Pope John Paul II declared that evangelization *"is not a matter of merely passing on doctrine but rather of a personal and profound meeting with the Savior."* I had gone through the motions with God, but never personally and profoundly encountered Him.

My vessel was actually vacant, shallow, and hollow inside – similar to those empty lamps. The Word of God hadn't come alive in my life. I wasn't living what my mouth was professing, even though I prayed many marvelous prayers and confessed profound elements of my faith every time I attended church. I only repeated the words from my head to fulfill my obligation and check them off my daily list.

I called God *"Lord"*, but I hadn't yet *made* Him Lord over every part of my life. What I knew in my head hadn't journeyed down to my heart and out through my hands.

Bottom line – I didn't *know* God. I was setting myself up for the ultimate regret in life: eternal regret.

1st **Step to No Regrets:** *Know God Personally.*

I had to graduate from talking it to walking it – not just on Sunday mornings, but every moment – every day – 24/7 – 365. The oil in the lamp is the Holy Spirit in my heart. That only comes from knowing God personally.

Chapter Two

The Heart of It All

> *"Come, let us return to the Lord! ...Oh, that we might know the Lord! Let us press on to know him! Then he will respond to us as surely as the arrival of dawn or the coming of rains in early spring. ...I don't want your sacrifices. I want you to know God; that's more important..."* (Hosea 6:1, 3, 6)

The foundation of my childhood faith helped form the person I am today. Without question, I wouldn't have recovered from the flash flood without it. From my rich Catholic upbringing and marvelous Jesuit high school training, my faith had a fabulous framework and skeletal structure; however, I had not yet grown meat on those bones.

I grew up in a blessed family heritage. As a cradle Catholic, I witnessed living models of faith all around me. My parents lived it personally through daily prayers, meal-time prayers, and family rosaries while driving in our VW Bus.

Several relatives dedicated their lives to serve Christ in lifelong vocations as nuns, priests, and brothers:

Sister Virginy cared for the poor, and Sister Maria helped the poor as a nurse in the inner-city; my great-uncle Vinnie was a Marianist brother who taught biology at the University of Dayton, and my great-uncle Clem was a priest for the Navajo Indians in Albuquerque, New Mexico, for over 50 years.

My grandparents did more than just talk about their faith. They walked it and daily lived it. They knew how to put meat on their skeletal framework of faith.

I witnessed my Grandma Rogers' profound faith in action as a music therapist helping veterans, amputees, and patients at hospitals. She *knew* God in a deeply personal way. As did Jesus, she poured out her life completely for others.

Grandpa Meyer delivered his popular horseradish to the Cincinnati delis down Queen City Avenue in a boxy blue truck. He often stopped along his route at church for Holy Communion or just to bask in God's presence for a few minutes. He deliberately lived his faith – to *know* God more personally every day – not just on Sundays – not just on Holy Days of "Obligation." He displayed daily devotion to God in big and little ways – doing regular stuff such as driving a delivery truck.

Even though I was encircled by living faith, I couldn't expect to just slide into Heaven on the coattails of my relatives. I couldn't claim their faith to convince God that I knew Him personally, too. If I continued their wonderful traditions for tradition's sake alone, it would merely amount to empty ritual. If I tried to rely solely on their faith and never made it personal, I would be a hollow vessel. I had to make it real myself.

I had to know God on a personal level.

God's Word hadn't taken root in me or developed muscles and flesh yet. I went through all the motions, but I didn't give God all my devotion.

I was merely a spectator at church, not a participant. All of the necessary elements were there, but I needed to energize, enliven, engage, activate, and awaken my faith by surrendering my life to Jesus in a personal way – myself.

My hunger and thirst for a passionate relationship with God led me on a spiritual journey of faith as a teenager that ultimately brought me to my knees in total submission to Him.

At that moment when my knees hit the hard floor, my heart hit the Rock of ages. I died to myself and fell in love with Jesus. His gift of salvation became complete in my life – when I fully received it and accepted Him as my Lord. It became real.

Whether we wish to face it or not, life is everlasting for all of us. We are going to live forever. The choice is whether it will be a joyful eternity in Heaven or a dreadful infinity of eternal regrets in hell: a never-ending separation and isolation from our Father God and our loved ones.

Deep within each of us, God placed a longing desire to be one with Him. It's a void that can only be filled by Him – such as a puzzle piece or a key that only God fits. Only He will satisfy; anything else is just a cheap imitation.

Just because we attend church doesn't automatically mean we know God personally. A lot of people love going to church, but aren't in love with Jesus.

Many people only know empty rituals and repetitive routines.

Growing up, I loved going to church. I knelt on the kneelers and prayed in the pew.

Yet, I didn't have a clue.

I wasn't in love with Jesus.

I didn't *know* God.

I didn't have an authentic, personal relationship with God. He doesn't just want a mandatory, obligatory hour once a week on Sunday morning where we "practice" our religion. He wants our life. He wants us to dwell in Him, share every moment together, and speak with us through prayer. As our Shepherd, He wants to teach us, delight in us, and even go through the floods and dark valleys with us. He can handle our frustrations, our anger, and our pain.

God is every bit almighty and powerful, and He's every bit personal and relational. We are created in His image.

God is real. He understands how it feels to be betrayed and beaten, despised and rejected, scourged and skewered by thorns and nails. Jesus groaned, wailed, and cried many times on earth. He understands our sorrows. God wants to hear our joys and our pains. We can be totally honest with Him and relate to Him in a real way.

When we know God personally, we can feel comfortable just venting, talking, and praying to Him in our normal, everyday voice. Start by just talking with Him from your heart.

In the Old Testament, Jacob wrestled with God all night – pleading for a blessing. At least he was honest and remained in contact with God.

After losing all ten children, his health, and his business, Job vented for nearly 35 chapters – on and on – while God remained silent. At least he was still talking honestly to God.

Countless times after the flash flood, I cried my eyes out to God and had some choice words with Him as I walked through our neighborhood, swayed on the swing sets on which my children played, and gazed up at the stars through my tears. I reminisced about our family memories and how life would never, ever be the same again. I wondered what I still had to live for.

Even though my emotions were scattered, my faith in God was still intact – because I already *knew* Him personally before that tragic moment in my life.

If I didn't *know* God – His voice, His Word, or His promises as true – I might not have made it through. At the time, I certainly didn't *feel* as if God had His arms of love wrapped around me every moment of every day. Yet, I *knew* He did because of our *relationship*.

Sometimes, faith means walking through the day and acting as if God must know what He's talking about. I may not always *feel* like it, but I *know* God's character enough to act in faith that somehow He is going to work it all out.

Through my pain after the flood, I knew that somehow God had a plan and purpose. I felt as if I was walking out on a limb and the only thing I had to hold onto was faith. The only way that's possible is to know God personally through a relationship with Jesus Christ.

This goes beyond just knowing about God. To know God means to delve to a much deeper level of intimacy, akin to the passion in Saint Paul's words when he cried out, *"Yes, everything else is worthless when compared with the priceless gain of knowing Christ Jesus my Lord. I have discarded everything else, counting it all as garbage, so that I may have Christ and become one with him. ...As a result, I can really know Christ and experience the mighty power that raised him from the dead."* (Philippians 3:8-10)

Moses echoed a similar passion before he set out on his journey, beseeching God, *"teach me your ways so I may know you and continue to find favor with you."* God granted his request and added, *"My Presence will go with you, and I will give you rest."* (Exodus 33:13-14 NIV)

God will grant you rest and peace when you know Him personally. Whether good times or bad, God desires our full attention and complete devotion. He may not cure, fix, or heal everything immediately, but the peace of His presence can pull us through the rigors, ruins, and remains of life.

The peace you seek only comes by *knowing* God in a personal way in honest relationship.

To nurture any relationship with someone you love takes a deliberate decision and continual, intentional effort. It is a lifestyle. It takes devotion, dedication, and commitment. It takes your heart. That's truly what God is getting at.

God wants your heart.

It just so happens that the heart of the matter – is a matter of your heart.

Jesus didn't save us just for Sundays. Christ didn't endure the crucifixion and die on the cross of Calvary just so we could attend church once a week. He gave His entire life for us and considers each of us worth dying for. Surely, we can consider Him worth living for.

In one of Jesus' final prayers with His Father before the crucifixion, He plainly said, *"And this is the way to have eternal life – to know you, the only true God, and Jesus Christ, the one you sent to earth."* (John 17:3)

It's a choice. It's simple. It's relational. It's personal.

Are you ready? Would you like to know God personally? Start by saying a simple prayer such as this.

"Lord Jesus, I come before You just as I am. I am sorry for my sins. I repent of my sins. Please forgive me. In your name I forgive all others for what they have done against me. I give you my entire self, Lord Jesus, now and forever. I surrender my heart, my will, and my life to you. I invite you into my life, Jesus. I accept you as my Lord, God and Savior. Heal me, change me, and strengthen me in body, soul, and spirit.

Come, Lord Jesus, cover me with Your Precious Blood, and fill me with your Holy Spirit. I Love You, Lord Jesus. I Praise You, Jesus. I Thank You, Jesus. I shall follow you every day of my life. Amen."

(Adapted from *"The Miracle Prayer"* by Reverend Peter Rookey, OSM).

If you prayed these words with all of your heart, then you personally committed and consecrated your life to Jesus.

Saying this prayer doesn't mean you're no longer a Catholic, Lutheran, Baptist or whatever denomination you claim.   It doesn't diminish or demean the wonderful treasures, traditions, prayers, or sacraments that are a part of your faith heritage. It enriches them.

You made a personal choice now to completely dedicate your life to Jesus. He is your Lord. You willingly declared a decision and are a fully devoted follower of Christ.

From this day forward, may your life be a vibrant, thriving relationship with Jesus. Become one with God as Jesus Himself prayed before He was crucified, *"My prayer for all of them is that they will be one...I in them and you in me, all being perfected into one."* (John 17:21, 23)

To know God personally takes both a decision and discipline. Each costs something. We *"will die for lack of discipline."* (Proverbs 5:23 NIV) So, it's worth it.

Nothing worth having comes free.

Jesus paid the ultimate price for our eternal salvation on Calvary.

Perhaps your decision to know God through Jesus Christ involved a miniscule amount of pain. Now, to maintain a discipline and know Him more may involve a bit more daily pain. You will have to surrender your life to Him and exchange your will for His.

The pain of decision and discipline may weigh a few ounces.

The pain of regrets – especially eternal regrets – weighs tons.

As in any close friendship, in order to know God personally, it is vital to cherish, cultivate, and care for that relationship daily. I'd like to offer three suggestions that have helped me.

First, pray. Pray always – everywhere, every day, and every way. Don't just carve out a couple minutes before work. That's a great start and very important. Don't relegate your relationship with Almighty God to merely a few morning minutes. Don't end your conversation there.

The moment we try to "make-room" for God in our day, we've already blown it. If we "squeeze God into" our day, we've missed it. We must give Him our whole day and our whole lives.

I do my best every morning to make sure my knees hit the floor soon after slipping out of bed. All over again, I daily commit my life and my day to God and ask that His Kingdom come and His *"will be done on earth, just as it is in heaven."* (Matthew 6:10) I want what He wants.

"…pray about everything. Tell God what you need, and thank him for all he has done. If you do this, you will experience God's peace, which is far more wonderful than the human mind can understand. His peace will guard your hearts and minds as you live in Christ Jesus." (Philippians 4:6-7)

Sit at the feet of Jesus, bask in His quiet presence, and listen to His Holy Spirit. When I do, a quiet assurance surrounds my soul with a peace that – no matter what happens today – God has it under His control. I know that nothing will happen to me that God won't first filter through His mighty hands.

This is what helped me heal so much after my family died in the flash flood. Because I knew God personally and took the time beforehand to build a relationship with Him through daily prayer, my faith was fortified when I needed it. I was able to run to Him – even with tears in my eyes and broken fragments of my heart in my hands. I was comfortable approaching the throne of Almighty God just as I was – shattered.

Somewhere deep within the caverns of my heart, I knew that God would be glorified through my pain and grief. I knew it because I knew Him.

Jesus plainly said, *"Here I stand at the door and knock. If you hear me calling and open the door, I will come in, and we will share a meal as friends."* (Revelation 3:20) Besides being Savior and Lord, He can also be our closest friend. God called Abraham a friend (James 2:23), as He did Moses (Exodus 33:17) – both of whom started out as ordinary guys who simply obeyed God and chose to spend time in His presence. They knew Him.

Rather than talk *to* God, instead, speak *with* God throughout the day. Listen to Him. Jesus said, *"My sheep listen to my voice; I know them, and they follow me."* (John 10:27 GNT)

My goal is to be slow to speak, quick to listen (James 1:19), and have ears to hear Him. Try more of "Speak, Lord, I'm listening" (1 Samuel 3:10) rather than "Hush, Lord, I'm talking."

"Listen to Him." (Mark 9:7)

"Pray at all times." (1 Thessalonians 5:17 GNT) Make your life a living prayer. By doing so, you will cultivate your relationship with Him. If you maintain this lifestyle, you will be amazed over time how much more deeply you know God.

Perhaps you just aren't comfortable approaching Almighty God. That's okay. Don't feel intimidated. Just speak honestly from your heart to Jesus as if He's right next to you.

Begin with just five minutes. Spend the first two speaking and the rest in silence...listening. Pray the Lord's Prayer (the "Our Father") slower than you ever have before. Chew every word and intend it with all of your heart. Then, thank God for three things. Tomorrow, mention three more. You'll never run out of things for which to thank God. Finally, because Jesus said, *"I will do whatever you ask for in my name,"* (John 14:13 GNT) pray with the words, "in Jesus' Name."

You'll be amazed how quickly five minutes in prayer flies by. Before long, it may turn into thirty minutes or more. Saint Francis de Sales rightly said about prayer, *"Half an hour's meditation each day is essential, except when you are busy. Then a full hour is needed."*

Next, read the Bible.

Besides knowing God through prayer, we can also know Him through Holy Scripture. His Words *"are spirit and life."* (John 6:63) Read the Bible daily so that His Words indwell within you and establish roots that remain.

To know God's Word is to know Christ. Jesus is the Word made flesh. (John 1:14) So, *"Ignorance of the Scriptures is ignorance of Christ."* (Saint Jerome, CCC 133) Indeed, *"In the beginning was the Word, and the Word was with God, and the Word was God."* (John 1:1 NIV) *"Heaven and earth will pass away, but my words will never pass away."* (Matthew 24:35 NIV) *"The Scriptures say, 'People need more than bread for their life; they must feed on every word of God.'"* (Matthew 4:4)

Every time Jesus was tempted by the devil in the desert, He struck down all three temptations using *"the sword of the Sprit, which is the word of God."* (Ephesians 6:17) He began each refute with the powerful words, *"It is written."* (Matthew 4:4, 7, 10 NIV)

If Jesus relied on His very own Word that much, how much more must we? God's Word is effective and gets things done.

"It is the same with my word. I send it out, and it always produces fruit. It will accomplish all I want it to, and it will prosper everywhere I send it." (Isaiah 55:11)

Sometimes we don't get it until we pursue it for ourselves. When we finally seek Him, it finally sinks in. (Jeremiah 29:13)

We have to choose.

This choice became so real to me through all of my family challenges with special needs, Down syndrome, miscarriages, adoption, and then death.

Each time life got tough, I always ran back to God's Word. I could not continue day-to-day without constant nourishment from Scripture. As I mourned heavily and grieved with endless tears, the power of His Word literally became life and breath to me.

At times when I buckled over so violently on the floor in my hollow home next to my empty bed, when my gut reeled with pain from crying with such severe convulsions, when I could barely gasp a breath through my spasms of tears – at times such as that – cracking open the sacred pages and dripping my tears upon the Scripture passages felt as if a paramedic placed an oxygen mask over my face.

Slowly, I could breathe again. Peace gradually flowed through my veins and into my heart.

That's truly how vital the Word of God became.

What I found astonished me. I felt content with Christ alone through His Word and His presence – even amidst the absence of my family.

I felt peace.

I gripped the pain and gradually worked through Post-Traumatic-Stress with my counselor as God restored my soul. Remarkably, I never experienced any depression or nervous breakdowns. I never touched addictions, substances, or delved into eating binges.

In my emptiness, I didn't run to the world. I ran to the Word.

In my anguish, I didn't run to the TV. I ran to the Almighty.

In my loneliness, I didn't run to the phone. I ran to His Throne.

I literally plunged myself into God's Word – reading it, devouring it, memorizing it, working it, and even reciting it out loud as I exercised and walked. In short, I lived it. It became a vital part of my being.

That's what gave me such hope and peace.

The Scripture promises wove threads through my frame that formed a fabric around my heart and tangibly manifested through my life.

After the flood, many people mentioned that I seemed to radiate God's countenance (Exodus 34:29) and exude His peace. Others didn't understand and thought I was in denial or had just lost it.

No, I found it! I found the Way, the Truth, and the Life (John 14:6), and He set me free from the shackles of misery. (John 8:36) I found it by knowing God personally even more deeply through His Words contained in sacred Scriptures.

Read the Bible every day as though it is oxygen for your body. Thirst for it. *"Search the Scriptures."* (John 5:39 KJV) Memorize them and recite them to yourself and your family. Cultivate an insatiable hunger and yearning desire for the Word. The more you read, the more you'll desire to read.

Since my teenage years, I grew to personally know God primarily by embedding His Word into my heart – by memorizing it. Scripture took root deep within and became a part of me.

Since then, I've compiled countless pages of Scriptures that help me draw closer to God. I even recite them when I exercise. So, when I pump the pedals, I also memorize Scripture. As I work my physical muscles, I also exercise and strengthen my "spiritual muscle" of faith.

The Word of God is *"alive and active."* (Hebrews 4:12 GNT) It never grows stale or old. The more we read and recite Scripture, the more we know God personally.

"No Bible – no breakfast, no Bible – no bed!"

My good friend, Father Larry Richards, declares this with great passion. It's a challenge that urges us to read the Bible at the beginning and at the end of every day. Read it after you wake up. Feed your soul before you feed your body. Then, let it be the last thing you read before you drift to sleep, so that it might penetrate your heart and thoughts for, *"on his law he meditates day and night."* (Psalm 1:2 NIV)

Embrace your day with God's Good News. You'll never regret it. *"Study this Book of the Law continually. Meditate on it day and night so you may be sure to obey all that is written in it. Only then will you succeed."* (Joshua 1:8)

The Bible is a large book and can seem a bit daunting at first. Don't feel overwhelmed, and don't try to read it all at once. To begin, start with the book of Psalms, the Gospel of John, or one the short letters in the New Testament (James, Philippians, or Colossians).

Finally, receive Holy Communion.

Regardless of what church or denomination you attend, nurture your personal relationship with God by receiving Holy Communion there regularly and reverently. As you do, vividly enter into the sacrifice Jesus made for you and offer your life as a living sacrifice to Him. If you are hurting or suffering, offer it up as a gift to God as you recall the sufferings Christ offered on the cross.

Countless times after the flash flood, I tearfully offered up my pain as I received Holy Communion. Though it was excruciating, I found healing: a bittersweet surrender in communion with the heart of God. It helped me to know Him more by literally sharing in *"the fellowship of His sufferings."* (Philippians 3:10 NKJV) Offering my pain to the honor of His Name mended and guided my heart along a path of healing.

In the Catholic faith, we are honored to share in the fullness of the Eucharist. We are presented the opportunity to know God intimately and become one with Christ's Body and Blood – soul and divinity – through the Blessed Sacrament of Holy Communion. In fact, *"Holy Communion augments our union with Christ. The principal fruit of receiving the Eucharist in Holy Communion is an intimate union with Christ Jesus."* (CCC 1391)

Many denominations share the privilege and rich tradition of regularly proclaiming Christ's death. I encourage you to embrace Communion with a greater passion of your union with Christ – to truly know Him through the sacrifice He gave. Approach it with great humility and reverence, not casually, flippantly, or unworthily.

Seize the opportunity to become one with Christ in a deeply personal way and know Him more. As the bread dissolves in your mouth and becomes one with you, offer your whole life to Christ and become one with Him.

Bringing It Home

Cultivate an intimate, personal relationship daily with Almighty God. To *know God personally* is the most important of all the 7 Steps.

If you know God personally through His Son, Jesus Christ, then the joys and beauty of this world are just the appetizer approaching Heaven. If you don't know God personally, then this world is the best it's ever going to get.

"And how do you benefit if you gain the whole world but lose your own soul in the process? Is anything worth more than your soul?" (Matthew 16:26)

Don't miss it. Don't risk not knowing God for eternity. *"Seek the Lord while he may be found; call on him while he is near."* (Isaiah 55:6 NIV)

Make the decision to know God through a relationship with His Son, Jesus Christ. After the decision comes the discipline. Discipline yourself as His disciple to walk with Him every day and know God more deeply – through continual prayer, Scripture reading, and Holy Communion. You will never regret it.

The pain of decision and discipline weighs ounces. The pain of regrets weighs tons.

You just made the first, most important step to your life of no regrets.

<u>Step 1 Action Points</u>

1) Make a no-regrets decision to *Know God Personally.*

2) Make a daily discipline to pray with God continually.

3) Make a daily discipline to read and memorize Scripture constantly. "No Bible – no breakfast, no Bible – no bed!"

4) Receive Holy Communion regularly and reverently.

Step 2
Chapter Three

Motions or Devotions?

> *"...true worshippers will worship the Father in spirit and in truth. The Father is looking for anyone who will worship him that way."* (John 4:23)

January 22nd, 1989: Super Bowl Sunday. I enjoy a good football game, though I'm not a full-tilt football fan. Still, I had crammed all week to complete my electrical engineering assignments at the University of Cincinnati just so I could pause for a few hours on Sunday afternoon and join the palpable fervor by television as the Cincinnati Bengals battled the San Francisco 49ers at Joe Robbie Stadium in Miami.

For weeks building up to today, the chants seemed to emanate from every station across Cincinnati's radio dial, *"Who dey think gonna beat them Bengals?"* The hype all around campus, the orange wigs, striped faces, and people dancing the "Ickey Shuffle" across the tri-state had reached a feverish pitch.

I had momentarily escaped my homework but could not escape the infectious energy of *the game* on television. The Bengals hadn't been in the Super Bowl since the days of Kenny Anderson and Cris Collinsworth years ago – when they lost to the San Francisco 49ers in 1982. Today, it was vindication time. It was *our* year.

I joined some of my engineering buddies in a dorm room with chips and pizza and was captivated by a cliffhanging, low scoring, classic football game as the Bengals toughed it out.

In the fourth quarter, with the 49ers trailing 16-13 and only 3:10 remaining, all of us Cincinnati fans gripped the edge of our seats by our fingernails – hoping the Bengals could hold onto their lead as Joe Montana began an unimaginable drive 92 yards away from the end zone. It appeared we had this one in the bag, as long as our defense could hold off Montana and his men.

Play by play, the 49ers confounded the Bengal defense. They gradually worked their way down the field with passes to the side, runs up the middle, and elusively effective plays. As our fingernails slowly slipped off the seats, John Taylor's sure hands made his only reception of the game as he caught a 10-yard touchdown pass. With only 34 seconds remaining to tick off the clock, the Bengals were socked a devastating loss of 20-16.

Everyone's hopes and dreams for vindication and a decisively stunning comeback were dashed. My buddies and I quickly shifted gears and returned to our engineering grind. A few days later, a paltry 3,000 disgruntled but loyal fans showed up to greet the losing team at Fountain Square in downtown Cincinnati as Ickey Woods danced one last shuffle.

What amazed me in the aftermath of *the game* was how dejected so many people were. They weren't just sad, but they were literally depressed – not just for a day, but for weeks and weeks. Even one of my engineering professors stopped right in the middle of a physics lecture. With long, stoic, mopey faces still staring into space in abject disbelief, he starkly said, "Look, everyone – it's just a *game*!" That didn't win him a lot of friends, but he was right. A game wasn't worth wasting an education.

Too many people had misplaced their devotion, adoration, affection – their worship – onto a team of men to fulfill their dreams and provide them hope, happiness, and contentment. Before the big game, I witnessed many people wearing football jerseys with men's names on them – star players who became their heroes. Human beings will always let you down (including me, especially). Anything other than God falls grossly short.

To fully live a life of no regrets, one name alone ought to be emblazoned across our life jerseys – *Jesus*. He is to be the banner of our hearts and our very lives. Our devotion, adoration, affection – our wholehearted worship – are to be directed solely to Him; *"...to love and worship him with all your heart and soul."* (Deuteronomy 10:12)

2nd Step to No Regrets: *Worship God Wholeheartedly.*

The deep yearning and longing of our hearts is to worship something real and lasting. That "something" can only be found in God alone.

We all strive to find someone or something to cheer. There's nothing wrong with that. God embedded it within us. Unfortunately, we often misplace and manifest it in sports games, music concerts, entertainment, fashion shows, or vices such as addictions or even food.

Worldly worship leaves us completely unfulfilled and empty.

Worshiping Almighty God feels like coming home.

It completes. It fulfills.

It fits our hearts flawlessly.

It's a perfect match – made in Heaven.

At last, our hearts can rest.

As Saint Augustine profoundly put it, *"Thou hast made us for thyself, O Lord, and our hearts are restless until they find their rest in thee."*

Only wholehearted worship of Him will lead you to a life of no regrets.

Just as I can't keep my body from yawning for more oxygen, so I can't keep my heart from yearning for more God. Our heart's hunger is an unquenchable longing to worship our Creator. *"I earnestly search for you. My soul thirsts for you; my whole body longs for you…"* (Psalm 63:1)

If I'm not worshipping God wholeheartedly, then I'm just living life halfheartedly, at best. My heart hasn't expanded to full capacity or filled completely with the air of God's breath.

God is seeking true worshippers. He doesn't deserve our halfhearted second or third best. He deserves our very best, utmost, and highest worship.

Until we do, we will likely find something or someone else to cheer. If we give God anything less than 100%, we will live to regret it. Our hearts will not be at peace.

God wants us exponentially more excited and unabashed about our worship of Him than the fervor on display at most sports games. God commands us all through the Bible to love Him with all of our heart, soul, and strength. (Deuteronomy 6:5, Deuteronomy 11:13, Matthew 22:37, Mark 12:30, Luke 10:27)

Are we willing to make that much racket and fuss over the God of the Universe? Are we willing to make fools of ourselves – in front of others – all for God? God deserves more than our leftovers.

We were made by God – for God. When we "prostitute" our worship and shift our adoration to other things or other people (Judges 2:12, 17), our hearts buck with restlessness (Acts 26:14) until we direct our worship back to God. It's essential to put first-things-first, deny ourselves, and surrender our stuff. Worshiping the God who made us brings peace to our souls and order to our chaos.

I discovered, particularly during times of trouble, that worry and fear soon dissolve as I set my heart fully on Him.

Seize time each day to thank and worship God wholeheartedly for His faithfulness, kindness, goodness, grace, mercy, and love. *"The eyes of the LORD search the whole earth in order to strengthen those whose hearts are fully committed to him."* (2 Chronicles 16:9) The prophet Hezekiah was one who *"sought his God wholeheartedly. As a result, he was very successful."* (2 Chronicles 31:21)

God's very first commandment tackles worship head on: *"I am the Lord your God… Do not worship any other gods besides me."* (Exodus 20:2-3) God couldn't make it much clearer. It's so easy to forget, because we're surrounded by distractions vying for our attention and stuff competing for our devotion.

"You must worship no other gods, but only the Lord, for he is a God who is passionate about his relationship with you." (Exodus 34:14) Are you passionate about your relationship with Him? Or do you devote more time to your phone, television, career, or hobbies? Do you give more devotion to your promotion, prestige, power, or position? God doesn't mind if we have things, but he minds if those things have us.

A few months after my family died, a good friend in Indiana offered me a short ride on his Harley motorcycle. What a rush! This particular sunny fall day, I just felt I needed to go hog-wild for a bit to clear my head. I sat behind him and held on for dear life. We blazed down county farm roads and several straightaways at 80 M.P.H. – leaving the autumn leaves in our dust. Whew! It cleared out my head alright – and a few other vital organs as well. When we safely pulled into the driveway, I felt as if my cheeks were pinned up against my ears.

I realized that God really doesn't mind if you drive a Harley – as long as that Harley doesn't drive you. That goes for everything.

For all of our stuff, there's a cost of ownership that can sap our devotion. God wants us to worship Him, not stuff. *"Friends, this world is not your home, so don't make yourselves cozy in it. Don't indulge your ego at the expense of your soul."* (1 Peter 2:11 THE MESSAGE)

It all boils down again to our hearts. The entire Bible is written as a love story. God is passionately in love with us and wants us to passionately love and adore Him through wholehearted worship.

Everyone is fanatical about something. Just take a quick snapshot of your life. Examine your calendar and your bank account. Where do you spend your time and your treasure? What occupies your thoughts? What do you constantly talk about? The answers to these questions speak volumes about your passion and what you worship.

Worship is all about the object of your adoration and affection. God wants that spot. He wants to be the center. When He is everything, then everything else falls into place. That imparts peace and enables us to live a life of no regrets.

The more deeply you know God personally, the hotter the flame burns to worship Him wholeheartedly. As King David proclaimed, *"Praise the LORD, I tell myself; with my whole heart, I will praise his holy name."* (Psalm 103:1) His worship came from within – inside out. It came from his heart. He didn't hold anything back, but rather blessed God with all that was within him.

Adoration is an attitude of the heart from within, not a feeling invoked from without. Music and other outward elements alone shouldn't pep, prompt, or provoke us to praise God. *"Man looks at the outward appearance, but the Lord looks at the heart."* (1 Samuel 16:7 NIV)

King David once openly made a public fool of himself for God. As the Ark of God was being transported back from the Philistines, the Bible says that *"David and all the people of Israel were celebrating before the Lord with all their might, singing songs and playing all kinds of musical instruments."* (2 Samuel 6:5)

Later, as they brought the Ark to the City of David, *"David danced before the Lord with all his might… with much shouting and blowing of trumpets."* (2 Samuel 6:14-15) When was the last time anyone made this much racket and fuss over excitement towards God?

Evidently, one of Saul's daughters noticed David's spectacle from her window and was filled with contempt for his foolish display. After she blatantly mocked him to his face upon his return, David retorted, *"I was dancing before the Lord… So I am willing to act like a fool in order to show my joy in the Lord. Yes, and I am willing to look even more foolish than this…"* (2 Samuel 6:21-22) He was unashamed and unapologetic.

King David was a true worshipper. He worshipped God wholeheartedly, with all of his might with no regrets. Saul's daughter, on the other hand, remained barren her entire life because of her remarks. Big regrets!

Whether or not you dance outwardly as King David, are you willing to make a fool of yourself for God? Do you love Him that much? *"If you are ashamed of me and of my teaching, then the Son of Man will be ashamed of you when he comes…"* (Luke 9:26 GNT, Mark 8:38 GNT)

I would rather be a fool in front of men and unashamed before God, than "keep my cool" in front of men and be ashamed before God.

What do you value and treasure? *"Wherever your treasure is, there your heart and thoughts will also be."* (Matthew 6:21) Life follows the same trajectory as your heart.

"Above all else, guard your heart, for it affects everything you do." (Proverbs 4:23) Let your heart beat wholeheartedly for God and He will direct your life.

We become like that which we adore. In other words, you are what you eat. You take on the character of whatever you spend your time around. Moses spent so much time in God's presence that he radiated God's glory. They had to cover his face with a veil just to gaze upon him. (Exodus 34:29-33)

The more we worship God, the more we reflect His nature. The more we worship stuff, the more we become like it – lifeless and sterile. *"Their idols are merely things of silver and gold, shaped by human hands. And those who make them are just like them, as are all who trust in them."* (Psalm 135:15, 18)

Abraham lived wholehearted worship. He waited his entire life for his dream to come true – to have a son. Finally, after nearly 100 years and several missteps along the way, he was blessed with his son, Isaac.

About 12 years later, God asked Abraham to sacrifice Isaac back to Him as an act of worship. Remarkably, Abraham never flinched. In fact, he got up *early* the next morning, chopped the wood, and set out to worship God wholeheartedly.

He had so much faith that, if necessary, he believed God would raise Isaac from the dead. (Hebrews 11:19) For, as he approached the mountain with his servants, he told them, *"The boy and I will travel a little farther. We will worship there, and then we will come right back."* (Genesis 22:5)

You might recall the rest of the story – how God stopped Abraham in mid-air, moments before the knife descended to slay his own son. The angel of the Lord exclaimed, *"...now I know that you truly fear God. You have not withheld even your beloved son from me."* (Genesis 22:12)

Abraham exuded the essence of wholehearted worship: don't hold anything back. Don't hold back your time, your treasure, your talent, or even your own flesh and blood.

After my family's funeral, I could have easily still held them back from God and others. Even from the very moment I identified their sacred, lifeless bodies, I surrendered each one with the words of Jesus on the cross, "Father, into Your hands I commend their spirits." I could have clung so tightly to their memories with bitterness that I might have never shared their story with others.

I could have shut down.

Instead, I opened up.

As Abraham, I chose to worship God by surrendering my right to hold onto them. They never belonged to me. They belong to God. Rather than clinch their memories tightly in my fist, I opened my hands and my heart to freely offer the legacy of their lives to help others *Know God and Live a Life of No Regrets*.

To this day, I strive to offer my life as a continual living sacrifice of wholehearted worship. Sharing my story over and over again is excruciatingly difficult. At times, I feel as if my heart bleeds within me. As Saint Paul insists, it's my reasonable act of worship.

"Therefore, I urge you…to offer your bodies as living sacrifices, holy and pleasing to God – this is your spiritual act of worship, your reasonable service." (Romans 12:1 NIV, KJV)

When you worship God wholeheartedly, don't hold anything back – not even your pain, your reputation, or your tears. Every element of your life can be a precious offering to God.

Once there was a sinful woman who came to Jesus with everything of value encased in an alabaster canister. She knelt, shattered it at Jesus' feet, and poured every drop of perfume upon Him as she wept. She risked her reputation even further by letting down her hair in public. When the perfume was gone, she dripped her tears upon Jesus' feet and wiped them with her hair.

As she served Jesus, those observing her indignantly insisted, *"Why this waste of perfume? It could have been sold for more than a year's wages…"* (Mark 14:4-5 NIV) This penitent woman understood that when you worship God wholeheartedly, it's an honor to waste all of your life's worth on Him.

Jesus was so impressed with her worship, that he called it a *"beautiful thing"* and declared that, *"wherever the gospel is preached throughout the world, what she has done will also be told, in memory of her."* (Mark 14:6, 9 NIV) That's the kind of wholehearted worship I desire to offer to God: the kind that He notices and sees as beautiful; the kind that is the same in public as it is in private; the kind that is a sweet smelling perfume to Him; the kind that changes the atmosphere in the room; the kind that is genuinely wholehearted – whether seen or unseen, and regardless of circumstance.

It's an attitude of our hearts, a posture of our souls, and a determination of our lives that we will worship God wholeheartedly no matter what everyone else thinks.

Three men in the Old Testament did just that. They worshipped God wholeheartedly in private and were tested in public. Their worship never once retreated. They refused to bow down to revere the king's false golden god. In doing so, they risked their very lives. Their conviction was that even *"If we are thrown into the blazing furnace, the God whom we serve is able to save us. He will rescue us... But even if he doesn't, Your Majesty can be sure that we will never serve your gods or worship the gold statue..."* (Daniel 3:17-18)

It cost them everything. The king threw them into the fiery furnace. In the end, God rescued them completely intact and unscathed. They were promoted. The dedication of their hearts changed the attitude of the king's heart to worship Almighty God alone. Their unwavering worship compelled the king to become a believer. That's no-regrets worship.

Chapter Four

Supreme Sacrifice

> *"Job...fell to the ground and worshiped. And he said: '...The Lord gave, and the Lord has taken away; Blessed be the name of the Lord.'"* (Job 1:20-21 NKJV)

The year following my family's funeral, I received word that Billy Graham was coming to Kansas City for one of his last Heart of America crusades. I've long admired his ecumenical message to draw men, women, and children of all denominations to the cross of Christ through a personal relationship with Jesus.

I volunteered for the mass choir to sing behind the platform for the three-day crusade. The first night, the skies opened up. Before the service began, Cliff Barrows, his faithful song-leader, rehearsed a few final hymns with us between the pelting raindrops. Having ministered for countless crusades across numerous decades, he articulated their unruffled attitude.

"Whether the weather be cold, or whether the weather be hot, we'll weather the weather, whatever the weather, whether we like it or not!"

Rain poured heavily most of the evening – except when Billy Graham spoke, ironically. Though our clothes were dampened, our spirits were not. Amidst the pouring rain, the worship team led us in the anthem, "Lord, I Lift Your Name on High." As my throat tightened, I worshipped along from the bottom of my heart as tears from my eyes collided with raindrops on my cheeks.

This was the last song my family and I sang in our minivan as it filled with water in the flash flood that fateful night. Now, singing it again in the rain in this stadium surrounded by a chorus of thousands was painful and yet powerful worship. It was surreal. It felt as if a canopy from Heaven descended upon us, as a warm, dry comforter amidst the cold, wet rain.

Through wholehearted worship, I felt a deep connection with my heavenly family and especially with God Almighty. This was worship akin to the woman who broke her alabaster jar. It was costly. It was painful. My heart was breaking all over again as my tears were flowing. Yet, it was fragrant as a sweet perfume.

Mercy Me performed "I Can Only Imagine", and I wept openly through the entire piece. I imagined my family in the presence of Jesus and how it would be when I see them all someday.

When you immerse yourself in God's presence through authentic worship, something amazing happens. As you bask in Him, you get to know Him even more – on a deeply personal level. As you understand the Creator of life more, you understand life more, for He made us in His image. As you comprehend better who you are in Christ, then your purpose, your destiny, and your reason for existence come into clearer focus. It answers a lot of life's most basic questions.

It's challenging enough just to get through life. Very few ever figure out who they are or discover their divine destiny. Knowing God personally and worshiping God wholeheartedly enable us to fulfill that lifelong quest with no regrets.

I still feel utterly inadequate when I minister through my story, even though I've shared it well over 800 times. I was trained in music, engineering, and business, but God led me into full-time ministry for over a decade. I find that in my weakness, God shows up. He is strong. He displays His power best through my frailty. (2 Corinthians 12:9) From the fractured fragments of my remains, from the pieces of praise I offer, He is able to weave together a newly-formed tapestry of patches and threads that possess a spectacular beauty all its own.

By offering my life as a living sacrifice to Him, I feel totally at peace – right in the palm of His Hand – as though I was created for such a time as this as my divine destiny. To live a life of no regrets, whatever you do, offer your life as an act of wholehearted worship to God.

A long time ago, a man named Job lost his ten children, his health, and his business – all at once. From the moment the messengers first delivered the horrific news to Job, he chose to worship God wholeheartedly. (Job 1:20-21)

Job remains the pinnacle and consummate role model of how to worship God wholeheartedly – regardless of circumstance. I discovered that my most acute worship often occurs amidst my most acute anguish. As Job did, I worshiped God immediately. Similar to the woman with the alabaster jar, I poured out my vessel completely until all I could offer Him was my tears.

The day after my family's funeral, I worshipped God from the keyboard at church with a song entitled "Mourning into Dancing." I had to publicly declare that I will still worship God with all of my heart, regardless of circumstance. I also felt as if I had to kick the devil in the teeth – particularly through that song – by not turning my back on God, but worshiping Him wholeheartedly instead.

A few weeks later, my brother and I attended a Promise Keeper's event in Kansas City. As thousands of men of all denominations stood together and sang in harmony of their love for God, the presence of God seemed to fill Kemper Arena with a tangible residue from Heaven.

During the worship songs, I leapt from my seat and headed down to the main floor near the band. As I approached the platform, a pain in my gut buckled my knees to the ground. I convulsed as a child in a fetal position, gushing forth with tears of worship and thanksgiving to God. I literally thanked Him right there for a life of no regrets with my heavenly family. I thanked Him for preserving my life on this earth for a purpose. I cried like a baby as I knelt in a ball. I didn't want the worship to end. The music wasn't entertainment. It was a means to convey our wholehearted worship to God.

As I drained myself of tears that evening, what I found floored me. I felt fulfilled. I felt peaceful. I felt incredibly cleansed, refreshed, and full of God.

Wholehearted worship kept me close to God and away from running towards worldly addictions. I never touched any of that rubbish. Especially at such a vulnerable moment in my life, I knew that nothing else would ever satisfy me except Christ. Worshipping God wholeheartedly is truly what saved me. It enabled me to continue living a life of no regrets.

Worship isn't just for Sunday mornings. It doesn't just "happen" during church when the songs are playing. Worship isn't an event, it's an attitude. Worship isn't just what we do, it's literally who we are. It's a way of life. We were created to glorify God.

So, I encourage you to recalibrate the attitude of your heart to offer worship to God out of every activity of your life: marriage, parenting, working, cleaning, commuting, eating, exercising, ministering, and loving. *"And you must love the Lord your God with all your heart, all your soul, all your mind, and all your strength."* (Mark 12:30) This is the foundation of wholehearted worship – loving God with all that is within us from the inside out.

My father lived most of his life in pain. With 24 surgeries – including four knee replacements, two shoulder replacements, and a pacemaker – his body was mostly spare parts. On top of numerous procedures to deal with complications from a lifetime of erosive osteoarthritis, he had a cancerous tumor removed from his lungs in 2009. After a six-month life expectancy, he valiantly and courageously battled stage-four lung cancer for 3½ years until he went Home in 2012 – two days after Christmas.

After 60 remarkable years of marriage, he was born to eternal life on the day of my mother's birth. In one of my final words with him, I thanked my father for giving his all and raising us so well. With a faint voice and barely able to speak, he muttered words that still resound in my heart: "It has been my honor, my son, Robert Thomas."

Through it all, my father never complained. He always thanked others: God, my mother, his family, church, neighbors, and caregivers. He was tough as nails with guts galore that made Superman look like a pansy. To manage the pain and persevere through it all, my courageous father offered it up to God as an act of worship. I miss him dearly and admire him more than any man I've known.

My father's attitude taught me volumes about patience, perseverance, and endurance for my own life. When I flash back to memories of my heavenly family and cringe in my gut every time I miss them, I offer it up to God as an act of worship. When my heart aches every time I share my story, I offer up my pain in wholehearted worship to Almighty God.

My mother taught in the Kentucky Public School system for 31 years. She educated the full range – from special-education to gifted students. For the last several years of her career, my father taught alongside her as an aide and assistant. As they taught practical lessons on life skills, job interviews, and budgeting, they spoke vividly about living life with passion from personal experience.

One method my parents used with their students to demonstrate living with passion was fun and vivid. With Dad sitting on a chair, Mom would nonchalantly walk by and mumble, "I love you" in a monotone voice, a deadpan look on her face, and a quick peck on the cheek. Not very convincing.

Then, they would do it all over again. Only this time, my mother would smack a smashingly juicy kiss on my father's lips, tilt him nearly all the way back in the chair, and passionately exclaim, "I love you!"   When asked, "Now, which would you rather have?" Dad would always emphatically declare, "The second one!"

Since we are made in God's image, surely He wants our passion for Him to be much like "the second one!" Instead, we brush by marvelous words such as, *"Our Father who art in Heaven, Hallowed be Thy Name."* We mumble through proclamations such as, *"Glory to God in the highest… We praise you, we bless you, we adore you, we glorify you…"* These words are brimming with Godly passion, but too often we recite them apathetically.

In nearly every sort of church service, multiple opportunities exist to express and enhance our worship. Don't breeze right by those worship moments and regret it. So often, it's easy to just tune out. Sometimes our bodies are present, but our hearts are absent. I've done it more than I care to admit. Sometimes I just coast through the service on auto-pilot, bored and devoid of passion. A deeply-rooted liturgy can be enriching and powerful, and yet it can also be a tempting opportunity to cruise through and tune-out of the service.

God wants our wholehearted worship to be full of passion. Yet, so often – before I personally knew God – I just mumbled wonderful words of worship and glossed over them with a glazed look across my face. If all I do is merely recite something I've memorized, it amounts to nothing.

"The Lord said, 'These people claim to worship me, but their words are meaningless, and their hearts are somewhere else. Their religion is nothing but human rules and traditions, which they have simply memorized.'" (Isaiah 29:13 GNT)

In several Gospels, Jesus referenced this verse from Isaiah, called the people *"hypocrites,"* and labeled their worship as *"a farce."* (Matthew 15:7-9, Mark 7:6-9)

Do I just consume a pew space on Sunday and merely fulfill an obligation? Or, am I consumed with love for God and fully filled by Him?

I could engage my whole heart and worship the God of the Universe who gave His life for me. Even though my stomach growls for lunch or my mind drifts toward the afternoon ball game; instead, I could offer my life as a living sacrifice to God.

Jesus already gave His life for me. The least I can do is offer my life to Him.

Even if finances are tight and more bills come in than dollars, my mind might be tempted to worry instead of worship. Worry and worship are really very similar actions. They both involve devoting my heart and attention to something.

Worry focuses on problems.

Worship focuses on God.

Worry accomplishes nothing.

Worship accomplishes great things because God inhabits our praises with His presence. (Psalm 22:3) In His *"presence is fullness of joy."* (Psalm 16:11 NKJV) Would you rather be full of God's joy, or full of worry's fear?

Worry and worship are also mutually exclusive. I can't do both simultaneously. If I focus on God and worship Him with all of my heart, then I can't possibly worry at the same time.

Thanking God for His goodness and loving-kindness consumes me in worship. When I passionately demonstrate my love for God through worship, it casts out the fear caused by worry. When I show God how much I trust Him by worshiping Him regardless of circumstances, situations, and storms that encircle me, then I've released the stranglehold of worry.

On the other hand, if I'm worried about who's going to win the big game or how I'm going to pay the big bills, I have no room left to worship God.

Worry has displaced worship.

The seeds of worry cannot take root in a heart of worship.

Neither can doubt, despair, or pity thrive amidst a thankful attitude of gratitude. That is the wonder of wholehearted worship.

Worship is also costly. My worship costs me everything. To deny ourselves and follow Christ is costly. It cost Abraham his son. It cost King David his reputation. It cost the three men in the fiery furnace their lives and reputation. It cost the woman with the alabaster jar her dignity and livelihood. In the end, God redeemed each one, including me, after choosing to worship Him wholeheartedly.

During his reign as king, David sinned against God by taking an unauthorized census. Afterwards, he asked forgiveness and was penitent. As a punishment, God sent a plague. Many innocent people died. David was mortified and wanted to accept full responsibility. He was advised to build an altar to the Lord.

When King David went to buy the land for the altar, the landowner was so honored that he offered to give it to David at no cost. He even offered oxen and wooden yokes to build the fire on the altar – all free of charge.

King David retorted, *"No, I insist on paying you for it. I will not sacrifice to the Lord my God burnt offerings that cost me nothing."* (2 Samuel 24:24 NIV)

God accepted his sacrifice and stopped the plague. King David understood that costly worship is a sacrifice that only you can make. Perhaps that explains why even Abraham – at over 100 years old – chopped the wood used to offer his own son. (Genesis 22:3) Any of his servants or even his strapping son, Isaac, could have easily swung the heavy axe that morning instead.

No one can worship for you. It must cost you something to be a sacrifice acceptable to God. That's why wholehearted worship must come from your whole heart. We will never experience complete peace in our lives until we get this right.

"So honor the Lord and serve him wholeheartedly. Put away forever the idols your ancestors worshiped… Serve the Lord alone. …choose today whom you will serve… But as for me and my family, we will serve the Lord." (Joshua 24:14-15)

The meaning of life is to know God, to love Him, and to serve Him. If we know God personally, we can't help but want to *"Serve the Lord with gladness."* (Psalm 100:2 NKJV) Serving God with gladness is the essence of wholehearted worship.

If you want to live a life of no regrets in every area of life, worship God with all of your heart. Surrender to

Him with reckless abandon. Don't resist or hold anything back. A life poured out is a life well lived. A life that worships God wholeheartedly is a life of no regrets.

Step 2 Action Points

1) Make a no-regrets decision to *Worship God Wholeheartedly.*

2) Make a daily discipline to worship God by serving Him with gladness (Psalm 100:2) and a thankful attitude.

3) Make worship a no-regrets lifestyle by offering every element of your life to God.

4) Spend time worshiping alone in quiet adoration of Jesus.

Step 3

Chapter Five

Perfect Peace

"Trust in the Lord with all your heart; do not depend on your own understanding. Seek his will in all you do, and he will direct your paths." (Proverbs 3:5-6)

"Son, this is where the rubber meets the road."

Moments before my father impressed these words on me, I had just faced the stark, wrenching reality that all four of my children perished in the flash flood.

The police asked me to give my first press conference. I clung to my father's every word of loving wisdom in the hospital. Every utterance that poured from his mouth felt like a balm of oil pouring over my head. They were sustenance to me after I identified the bodies of my dear children only a few hours earlier.

Search crews were still desperately trying to find Melissa. All of our extended family members were still grasping for hope in the bleak white waiting room on the second floor of that Kansas hospital in September of 2003.

My father continued. "Don't hesitate to say how you still trust God. This is where we either believe what we say or we don't. Either God is God, or He is not."

As my father and I grappled with what to express at the press conference, his words of wisdom took root deep within my heart. Those wise words from my father still ring true today.

Either we trust God, or we don't.

Either God is God, or He is not.

Either we believe our faith, or we don't.

It's simple, but it's not easy.

If we trust God, then we must do so absolutely, 100% and without question – regardless of how bad life gets. When we surrender our lives to Christ, He doesn't owe us any explanations. After all, *"It is God's privilege to conceal things."* (Proverbs 25:2)

I had buckets full of questions for God at that moment. I do to this day. Still, God's responses to me have been devoid of answers and reasons.

Instead, God's Words to me in Scripture have been full of hope and the challenge to simply trust that He knows what He's doing.

"You will keep in perfect peace all who trust in you, whose thoughts are fixed on you! Trust in the Lord always, for the Lord God is the eternal Rock." (Isaiah 26:3-4)

Do I really, fully, truly trust God with all of my heart? Can I trust Him so much that I don't rely at all on my own understanding? Can I fully experience perfect peace – especially now – if I simply fix my thoughts on Him?

How can an electrical engineer set aside my rationalization, reason, and logic? That's a tall order for a practical, pragmatic guy, particularly to think that if I seek God in everything I do, He really will direct my paths.

Up until the flash flood, our family sought God diligently in every conceivable aspect of our lives: parenthood, marriage, adoption, special-needs children, finances, tithing, working, and everyday life.

Did the same God direct our paths that fateful night to place us smack-dab in the epicenter of a flash flood in Kansas of all places? How in the world does that happen? Is God truly sovereign in all these sorts of details?

Does this litany of questions strike a chord? When life happens, is your glut of questions echoed by a vacuum of answers? That's precisely where trusting God comes in: when nothing around you seems to add up.

3rd Step to No Regrets: *Trust God Absolutely.*

A life of no regrets trusts God even when He doesn't make sense and takes us along a path that is terrifying, baffling, and perhaps even excruciating.

Trusting God absolutely – regardless of life's confounding circumstances – is actually a deeply rooted act of faith and worship, especially amidst life's perplexing situations. It proves you love Him enough to surrender your life entirely into His hands.

Trusting God means faith in action.

Trusting God means to free-fall into the arms of Jesus.

Trusting God means to walk out onto a limb when the only thing you've got to hold on to is faith.

That's what Job declared after he lost all ten of his children. He still emphatically declared, *"Though He slay me, yet will I trust Him."* (Job 13:15 NKJV) In other words, even if it kills me, I'm still going to trust God.

If Job hadn't placed his trust in God, if he continued a nonstop barrage of complaints and criticisms over how unfair life is, then I'm convinced he never would have been blessed with ten more children, double of everything else, or even 140 years of a full life, enjoying four generations of his children.

Imagine just the opposite if Job hadn't trusted God. Imagine the lifelong regrets he might have carried. Imagine all of the countless people who wouldn't have been inspired by his faith.

That's the choice you and I have every day. Do we trust God or not? Regrets or no regrets? Do we trust God when the bottom falls out, when the car breaks down, when the light turns red, when the milk goes sour, when the meeting goes south, when the job goes away, when the bill collectors come, when they padlock the doors, when the disability becomes impossible, when the divorce papers come, when the diagnosis arrives, when our children turn away, when the storm hits, when the floodwaters devastate, or even when our loved ones die?

Do you trust God when life happens?

Will you?

One of the most difficult things for me to do after the flood was trust God again – after He let me suffer so much. Because I knew God personally and had established a relationship with Him, I knew He wouldn't let me endure such worldly pain if He didn't somehow intend it for such eternal gain.

When my world was washed away, I was traumatized, but I was not paralyzed. I was inundated, but not devastated. That's because – by the grace of God – my faith was already active, alive, and fortified. I still had a life because it was built on the Rock of Jesus Christ. (Matthew 7:25) I could still function because I still trusted God absolutely.

In the hospital that first night, even before I knew anything about my family, while shivering under the blankets in that lonely hospital bed with Melissa's brother praying by my side, I uttered a prayer of Divine Mercy, "Jesus, I trust You." It was a simple prayer, but a profound statement of faith. It meant that whether they found my family alive or deceased, I was still going to trust God. Either way, I knew they were okay. I knew Jesus' promise that, *"My sheep listen to my voice; I know them, and they follow me. I give them eternal life, and they shall never die. No one can snatch them away from me."* (John 10:27-28 GNT) I believed that even if their bodies died, they didn't truly perish for eternity.

I had peace.

Even then.

Still now.

Because I actively choose to trust God through it all, I'm able to live a life of no regrets and even experience "perfect peace" amidst everyday adversity.

Jesus epitomized perfect peace when he slept in the back of the boat with his head on a pillow through the fierce storm that rocked the disciples' faith. (Mark 4:35-40) He was still fully a man, but He fully trusted God so absolutely that He could sleep in the middle of the chaos – as though He was sheltered in the eye of the hurricane. That's where He wants us – amidst the storm – trusting Him in perfect peace.

Jesus poignantly asked the disciples, *"Where is your faith?"* (Luke 8:25) They chose to put more faith in the wind, the waves, and the storm than in the One who created them all and was right there with them in the boat.

Throughout Scripture, God asks us simply to trust Him even when we can't see or don't understand.

Trusting God assumes risks, but instills peace.

"…his heart is steadfast, trusting in the Lord. His heart is secure; he will have no fear." (Psalm 112:7-8 NIV) That aptly describes Jesus' sleep in the boat: secure, steadfast, and no fear. That's how I strive to respond under pressure.

The key is to keep our thoughts *"fixed on"* Him. (Isaiah 26:3) I understand how difficult it can be to fix your eyes on Jesus when they endlessly overflow with tears. More than once I was tempted to try a quick fix. Rather than chuck it all, I clung to my faith with my fingernails. I clutched my Bible and cracked open its pages of life.

Our eyes and hearts will swiftly drift elsewhere if they aren't locked on the Lord – especially during difficulties. Something will uselessly try to fill the emptiness in our mind and the brokenness in our heart. I knew nothing else would work. So, choosing discipline over emotion, I kept my thoughts fixed on Him by focusing on His Word. I ran to the Bible and read it constantly. Truly, Scripture saved me. Jesus – the Word incarnate – saved me.

Displaced trust leads to regrets because anything or anyone other than God will eventually let us down. Only Christ is enough. That's why it's vital to establish a discipline of running to God by nourishing a personal relationship with Him through prayer, reading Scripture, and wholehearted worship.

After the flash flood, countless people remarked how God's peace seemed to be all over my countenance. It was real and still is – because of Him, not me. As I recall the vivid details of that night, somehow I had no fear through it all.

I was shaken and shattered, but I was undergirded with the peace of God. I somehow had a deep sense that He had it all totally under control. It was too monumental to be anything else. I had faith that God wouldn't let this happen unless He was going to bring us through it. I had peace. I trusted God absolutely.

I still had a glut of grief, emotions, and questions. My faith didn't just zap it all and evaporate it away. Much like Job, I found that God could handle my questions and confusion. My honest, raw emotions with Him demonstrated that I could still trust Him with my fractured heart. He could handle it.

In fact, as I ran to Him, it almost seemed that God welcomed my tears and frustrations because it fostered a deeper dependency and intimacy. Wrestling with God kept me in contact with God.

My honesty with God helped me to keep my faith because I ran to Him and not to addictions. I clung to His Word. I chose not to be bitter or resentful. I chose not to remain a victim my entire life. Although every fiber of my flesh fought against it, I chose to trust God.

In the months and years that followed, in my hollow home that echoed my family's voices, in the wee-night hours as I drenched my pillow with tears, I discovered that I could still trust God. He still had my heart.

I came to the end of me and tapped into the essence of His remarkable grace. Even when it seemed as though God was the most absent, He was actually the most present.

Sometimes God even seems to withdraw from us for a season to test our faithfulness amidst adversity. Even then, we must remain faithful and trust Him absolutely.

"…God withdrew from Hezekiah in order to test him and to see what was really in his heart." (2 Chronicles 32:31)

"Until the time came to fulfill his word, the Lord tested Joseph's character." (Psalm 105:19)

"Don't be afraid of what you are about to suffer. The Devil will…put you to the test… Remain faithful even when facing death…" (Revelation 2:10)

Let's face it, life is a test. People were tested throughout the Bible. We are tested throughout life. The question is, "How do we respond?" With no regrets? By trusting God absolutely? Abraham did when God asked Him to sacrifice his son, Isaac. Abraham didn't delay, but he *"was trusting God so much that he was willing to do whatever God told him to do. His faith was made complete by what he did – by his actions."* (James 2:22) That's absolute trust. That's putting muscle to your faith, because *"...faith without actions is dead"* (James 2:26 GNT) and *"No one can please God without faith."* (Hebrews 11:6 GNT)

Living out real faith through absolute trust is a daily decision. Every morning as my knees hit the floor, I surrender my heart, my will, and my life saying, "Lord, I trust *your* will – even if it might be painful, even if it may not be the way I would choose. I still trust you absolutely."

I find myself repeating this throughout the day – as I drive, exercise, work – or wherever I am when challenges and decisions surface. I just whisper a simple prayer, "Lord, I trust you in this. I commit it into your hands."

It's simple faith in action. I believe it speaks volumes to God Almighty.

Chapter Six

Greater Good, Greater Glory

"Trust me in your times of trouble, and I will rescue you, and you will give me glory." (Psalm 50:15)

When we trust God absolutely, I believe it rises as a prayer to Heaven, becomes magnified through a megaphone, and resonates as a sweet sound in our Father's ears.

Trusting God gets His attention.

Absolute trust declares that God's way is the best way, even though it's not always my way.

The way God rescued my family and me from the flash flood surpasses the way I would have preferred. I wanted the waters to recede that night so we could safely dry off, tow our minivan, and continue with our thriving family.

God rescued my family in a different fashion. They got to go to Heaven. What better place is there? Who is more blessed? Being washed up on the shore as the sole survivor was certainly not my idea of God rescuing me. It felt like a cruel joke. It felt like torture.

Nobody asked me. I asked God to assume full control. I trusted Him absolutely.

Evidently, the purpose of God's way is to bring Him more glory. Somehow – when we trust God absolutely – He blends all of our pain in a mixing bowl of life and ultimately works it all out to bring glory to Him, blessings to others, and grace to us. *"All of these things are for your benefit."* (2 Corinthians 4:15)

That's truly a life of no regrets – to invite God to bring glory through your story, without bucking or resisting His will. For, *"We know that in all things God works for good with those who love him…"* (Romans 8:28 GNT)

Remember the blind man whom Jesus healed along the roadside? His disciples were wondering why the man was born blind in the first place and whether it was brought about by sin. *"Jesus answered, 'His blindness has nothing to do with his sins or his parents' sins. He is blind so that God's power might be seen at work in him.'"* (John 9:3 GNT)

Remarkable.

Jesus used one man's story to display God's glory.

He used one man's pain to glorify His Name.

He used one man's infirmity to display His divinity.

Saint Paul put it this way. *"And this small and temporary trouble we suffer will bring us a tremendous and eternal glory, much greater than the trouble."* (2 Corinthians 4:17 GNT) You might disagree that your trouble is *"small and temporary."* I can relate. I believe Paul is saying that compared to the tremendous glory God will bring, your trial will eventually seem *"small and temporary"* as you look back on it one day.

Saint Peter also urges me not to be caught off guard or surprised by tests and trials as though they are out of the ordinary, but to *"...be glad that you are sharing Christ's sufferings, so that you may be full of joy when his glory is revealed."* (1 Peter 4:12-13 GNT)

Notice a pattern emerging? When we trust God absolutely, He uses our suffering for a greater good and a greater glory. The ultimate example is the greatest good that came from Jesus' suffering and death on the cross — salvation for our souls.

After my family died, I honestly couldn't fathom what good might possibly come forth. I believed God could and would, but I had no idea how. How could God bring it about from something so dreadfully excruciating?

Almost immediately after my simple hospital prayer declaring, "Jesus, I trust you," my tribulation started bringing transformation into people's lives. By the grace of God, it renewed people's faith, it drew them to the cross of Christ, and it drew people closer to their families.

One man approached me and declared, "Now I know which of my two job offers to choose, because I want to have no regrets with my family." Another couple exclaimed, "After hearing your story, we want to keep having children." Another man remarked, "That's the single most powerful testimony I've ever heard. Now I'm going to pray daily with my wife."

After attending my family's funeral and being impacted by my special-needs daughter from China, another family made the pilgrimage there and adopted a beautiful girl. We became dear friends since then and, after nearly three years alone in my empty home near Kansas City, they purchased my house. Now, their beautiful four children have brought life brimming back and turned it into a vibrant home.

One Sunday morning, a father heard my story at a church service. He ran home and brought his teenage son to the second service. Afterwards, I hugged their necks, prayed with them, and learned a day later that his son averted suicide within moments of hearing me. Evidently, that very weekend marked the first anniversary of a tragic automobile accident where several friends died in his car. After an excruciating year of guilt and anguish, the boy had lost his will to live. After hearing God's grace through my story, he discovered a new purpose in life and wanted to start serving others by sharing his story.

Do you trust God absolutely? These are real stories of real people whose lives have really been forever changed, transformed, and even saved by the grace of God – all because He continues to use redemptive suffering to bring great glory and greater good. These are just a handful of countless people whose testimonies alone would overflow this book.

No regrets.

If God can bring this through my story, imagine what He can bring through you – if you trust Him absolutely enough to allow Him.

If I hadn't made that simple pivotal decision to trust God absolutely, imagine how different the outcomes might have been. Try to imagine the complete opposite. My life would have been a wreck and useless for God. Other lives, marriages, and families might be worse off right now. At least one orphan that we know of might still be without parents in China.

This is real stuff. This is powerful. This is life. This is God.

What do you choose?

Will you choose to trust God absolutely?

When we don't trust God absolutely, then our suffering is wasted and only intensifies over time. It worsens as our problems compound with no apparent goodness in sight. Furthermore, we withhold blessings from God, others, and from ourselves. Big regrets!

"For the sadness that is used by God brings a change of heart that leads to salvation – and there is <u>no regret</u> in that! But sadness that is merely human causes death." (2 Corinthians 7:10 GNT)

When my father was 18 years old, about five years before he ever met my mother, he enlisted in the Army for two years as a Private First Class with the 9th Infantry Division stationed at Fort Dix in New Jersey. He patriotically desired to serve his country, yet he also wanted to fulfill his passion in broadcasting and ultimately raise a family. Since television was still maturing and just coming to fruition, he didn't want to miss that window of opportunity in its early years – in the event that he was drafted for an indefinite period.

By the grace of God, Dad's two years of service ended within two weeks of the start of the Korean War.

One of Dad's Army buddies was sent to Korea within several weeks after the war started. Only a few weeks later, he was killed in combat. My father could have been killed right alongside him. If Dad had originally enlisted for a three-year stay, or if he was drafted instead, I likely would have never been born and you might not be reading this right now.

Do you trust God's sovereignty absolutely – to manage the most miniscule details of life? *"The Lord works out everything for his own ends."* (Proverbs 16:4 NIV)

God is in the details of life – when we surrender control of our lives over to Him. *"When you bow down before the Lord and admit your dependence on him, he will lift you up and give you honor."* (James 4:10) God invented time and cares about it – down to the very second.

Recall when Jesus' dear friend, Lazarus, became deathly sick. Without question, Jesus cared deeply for him. His love for Lazarus is mentioned three times in one chapter. However, when Jesus received word of Lazarus' illness, He didn't even budge. In fact, He stayed put for two more days.

Isn't that peculiar? You would have thought the Savior of the World would bolt right over to Bethany to save the day or even heal Lazarus from afar. Jesus promised, *"The final result of this sickness will not be the death of Lazarus; this has happened in order to bring glory to God, and it will be the means by which the Son of God will receive glory."* (John 11:4 GNT) Once again, Jesus utilized death and suffering to glorify God, the Father, and Himself.

Strangely, when the disciples alongside Jesus balked at his judgment to linger rather than leap to Lazarus' side, He plainly explained to them, *"Lazarus is dead, but for your sake I am glad that I was not with him, so that you will believe."* (John 11:14-15 GNT) Hmmm. Does His statement seem odd? It still amazes me and, at the same time, it bothers me every time I read it. Jesus was actually glad that He wasn't there and allowed Lazarus to die. Whoa! Was He also glad that my entire family died one night in a flood? Was He glad for your suffering or loss? Was He glad He didn't show up and save the day? Man that hurts. On the surface, it sounds quite calloused.

Embedded in Jesus' words are how the *"final result"* would *"not be the death of Lazarus."*

God had a plan – a good one.

When you're buckled in pain, perhaps the last thing you want to hear from someone trying to console you is, "Well, I guess God had a reason. It must be His will."

Grief and pain are very unsettling. We struggle to find comforting words to say. None of us can imagine how others feel. We can't compare pain. Each loss is uniquely devastating. Sometimes your heart and mind just aren't ready for a big-picture perspective yet. All you want is for someone to hold you and listen. Fewer words are often better.

When Jesus arrived in Bethany, He consoled Lazarus' sisters, Martha and Mary. *"I am the resurrection and the life. Those who believe in me will live, even though they die; and those who live and believe in me will never die."* (John 11:25-26 GNT)

He spoke to their immediate needs with reassuring truth. He didn't require them to try to see the big picture yet. They were still grieving in terrible anguish and probably weren't ready to hear anything else.

Earlier, He had let the disciples in on a secret about how the *"final result…will be the means by which the Son of God will receive glory."* When we trust God absolutely, this is our hope and assurance. The final result of all the pain will bring glory to God.

On August 30, 2004, one of our two dogs was missing. I hopped on my bike, searched all around the neighborhood, and did everything I could to find him, but never did. Amadeus was gone – exactly one year after my family died.

He was a scruffy cocker-spaniel from our California days. Amadeus was loyal and loveable with our children and meant even more to me since their deaths.

He and our feisty rat-terrier, Ira, accompanied me on neighborhood walks alone. When I came home, they cheerfully greeted me with the kind of comfort only canines can. Both dogs provided some much needed laughs and living reminders of family memories.

Then, about a year after Amadeus disappeared, a neighbor's rare breed of ferocious attack dogs were untied and pounced through our fence after Ira. He barked hysterically, but was outsized and outnumbered. I rushed out to scatter them, but it was too late. As I approached, one of the two dogs ran away with Ira snatched in its mouth.

I was mortified.

"No!" I screamed at the top of my lungs. "Get off him!"

I chased them down the street. The dogs vanished. Their owner was gone, his house empty. My neighbors and I searched far and wide for Ira to no avail.

Many months later, I started smelling a stench in the basement near a window. I figured it was a dead mouse or something. I grabbed a chair and peered through the dusty glass into the shallow window-well. I vaguely saw something white outside. I went out and army-crawled under the deck amidst the dirt and leaves with a flashlight. I found a few toys Zachary apparently hid there. A little further, in the window well, was the white fur of Ira's remains. He must have hobbled back home and huddled out of sight to die.

Amadeus wandered away. Ira died a bizarre, brutal death. Our two dogs were the last living connections to my family. I ran out to the back yard, fell to my knees in the dirt, looked up to Heaven, and cried out to God.

"Come on, God. Must I lose everything alive in my life? What do you want from me? What must I do to follow you?"

My tears flowed as I clutched the grass and sensed God's presence around me. I recalled Saint Paul's words. *"I have been crucified with Christ. I myself no longer live, but Christ lives in me. So I live my life in this earthly body by trusting in the Son of God, who loved me and gave himself for me."* (Galatians 2:19-20)

Following Christ meant that I must completely and absolutely surrender every living part of me and depend fully on Christ to live through me. I still had to trust Him absolutely.

Joseph in the Old Testament did. His older brothers threw him into a pit and sold him into slavery. Joseph was wrongfully accused and imprisoned for many years until God finally worked it all out. Joseph never stopped trusting God, even after life was unfair to him for over ten years. In the last book of Genesis, Joseph reconciled with his brothers and declared, *"As far as I am concerned, God turned into good what you meant for evil."* (Genesis 50:20)

Even Job – who lost nearly everyone and everything closest to him – was ultimately restored with a blessed life: ten more children, double of everything else, and healing through his sick body. He continued to trust God absolutely. After he endured his suffering with remarkable patience, *"the Lord's plan finally ended in good, for He is full of tenderness and mercy."* (James 5:11)

God is a God of good endings.

God is tender and merciful. He really isn't mad at you. He's mad about you. He genuinely cares about you. He loves you. God will bring goodness, grace, and glory through your painful story – when you trust Him absolutely. Someway, somehow, out of your mess, He can bring forth a message – to encourage someone else in need.

If he can do it for Job, he can do it for you. He's done it for me in ways I never could have fathomed. He wants us to dream again and know that life is still worth living – because He conquered death and destroyed its grip on us.

"You have allowed me to suffer much hardship, but you will restore me to life again and lift me up from the depths of the

earth. You will restore me to even greater honor and comfort me once again." (Psalm 71:20-21)

Though it may not always seem true, God has your best interest and His greatest glory in mind. He's got it all worked out together – in perfect unison.

It took me several years and much professional counseling after the flood before I felt ready to make my heart vulnerable again. I wasn't seeking a spouse or a family. I focused on seeking God.

I remembered a verse in the Bible that if I pursue God first, then He will give me all that I need. (Mathew 6:33) If God wanted me to marry again, He was going to have to bring a gracious woman into my life miraculously. Besides, I thought, "Who would ever want to consider a guy like me with a past like mine?"

Through a divinely ordained series of events, I was introduced to a girl from Indiana named Inga. She was delightfully stunning with golden hair, an infectious smile, beautiful golden-green eyes, and large eyelashes to match. As we grew to know one another, she asked to visit Kansas City to come face-to-face with my previous life. She wanted to experience my past to help understand me better.

Inga asked detailed questions, and I spared no memories as they came to mind each milestone along the way. As we retraced the path of the flash flood, we walked nearly four miles along Jacob Creek for six hours. We knelt by each sacred location where the search crews had found my family members. We reverently sang a verse of the hymn "We Are Standing on Holy Ground" at each site, said a prayer, and placed a rose on the soil.

It was a seminal, defining moment between us. It demonstrated Inga's compassion for my heavenly family, her respect for me, and the sheer magnitude of her courage to face something so daunting and potentially overwhelming.

She wasn't intimidated by my family's memories. She was interested in them. She encouraged me to keep reminiscing because the more she knew about them, the more she knew about me. Her calm, cool, and confident spirit demonstrated how grounded she was in her upbringing of faith and family. She never tried to squelch me from bringing up the past. She accepted it, realizing that it will forever be a part of who I am.

I was amazed by Inga's simple yet profound faith. I thought, "Is she for real?" I brought her to Cincinnati for Thanksgiving and introduced her to my family. My parents instantly took to her and saw how she brought a smile to my face, a bright glimmer to my eyes, and a new spring in my step.

Inga's simple outward splendor was stunning, but so was her inward beauty. It came from her *"true inner self, the ageless beauty of a gentle and quiet spirit, which is of the greatest value in God's sight."* (1 Peter 3:4 GNT)

Although we hadn't said the words yet, I sensed that Inga loved me and that I deeply loved her. When I profess my love, it's something that I'm not ashamed to shout from the mountain tops. So, on Valentine's Day, I stood up on a bench in full view of Inga and all the restaurant patrons, and professed with all my might:

"Inga, I've waited a long time to say this and you've patiently waited for this moment. So now, in front of God, all of Heaven, your family and everyone here, I want to finally say…I am passionately in love with you! Inga Elizabeth, I love you. And, with my love, I give you all of my heart."

Later, early one Friday morning, I ascended a ladder to her bedroom window and tapped on the screen. Could this be happening? It was like a fairytale.

"Good morning, Gorgeous!" I exclaimed. "I have something for you." I handed her a brimming bouquet of orange roses with one hand and reached into my pocket with the other.

This was the time. Joy was coming. Because I trusted God absolutely even through my season of weeping, He brought joy this morning. *"Weeping may go on all night, but joy comes with the morning."* (Psalm 30:5)

"I need to ask you something. May I come in?" Without hesitation, she exclaimed, "Sure!"

We made our way to the piano as I unfolded a song I composed and serenaded her with a new melody.

With the music still sustaining in mid-air, I scooted off the piano bench, knelt down on one knee in front of her, pulled the diamond ring out and asked, "Inga, will you marry me?"

"Yes, Robert. You bet, I will."

Our holy wedding in May 2006 was a sacrament, a covenant, a commitment, a prayer, and a display of redemption – all at once. It was a miraculous moment to behold. *"Then I bowed my head and worshiped the Lord. I praised the Lord…because he had led me along the right path to find a wife."* (Genesis 24:48)

We kissed as husband and wife while a burst of spontaneous applause erupted as we gleefully recessed down the aisle.

"For the winter is past, and the rain is over and gone. The flowers are springing up, and the time of singing birds has come... For love is as strong as death... Many waters cannot quench love; neither can rivers drown it." (Song of Solomon 2:11-12, 8:6-7)

We hugged everyone's necks on the church steps and passed out 150 colorful balloons. Inga and I held one together that aptly read, *"With God, all things are possible"* (Matthew 19:26 NIV) with a note from both of us to my heavenly family. On the count of three, we released a dazzling array of balloons to Heaven accompanied by our love, our thoughts, and our thanks.

Somehow, God divinely ordained this beautiful marriage to come out of the ashes of my life. Ours is truly a match made in Heaven. As God said to Abraham, *"Is anything too hard for the Lord?"* (Genesis 18:14)

God can truly work all things ultimately for our good. He can and will redeem our lives, our pain, and our suffering if we place our trust in Him. If God can do this for me, imagine what He can do for you.

Will you trust God absolutely?

<u>Step 3 Action Points</u>

1) Make a no-regrets decision to *Trust God Absolutely.*

2) Make a daily discipline to keep your thoughts fixed on God amidst tribulation; allow His peace to drown your fears.

3) Make a daily discipline to trust God throughout life's unexplainable tests and trials.

4) Don't waste your pain, but trust God enough to redeem it with His glory in His good time.

5) Trust God's hand to direct your plan, even when you don't understand.

Step 4
Chapter Seven

Do What, When, Because...

> *"If you love me, obey my commandments."*
> (John 14:15)

"Son, do *what* you're told, *when* you're told, *because* you're told."

Period.

I heard this phrase countless times growing up as my parents taught us to obey.

I knew that if any other utterance slipped out of my mouth – if I didn't fully obey at that precise moment – the consequences would be painful and unpleasant.

When our entire family went to church, we filled a whole pew. Getting all eight children to behave for an hour was a challenge all its own. Usually, each of us had an episode where we goofed off, mouthed off, or misbehaved...once.

When that happened, Dad didn't use words.

He lovingly and promptly picked us up, marched out the door, and disciplined us. We cried our eyes out. We knew we had willfully crossed the line. My father embraced us afterwards as we sobbed in his arms. Each of us acted up in church one time. It never happened again. We learned what it meant to obey.

My parents had to run a tight ship. We were never permitted to talk back to them. We were never allowed to cross the street or even play near it without holding their hands. We were never permitted to swim in the ocean without our lifejackets until we could prove our aquatic abilities at the YMCA. Often, we were the only ones on the beach wearing life jackets. At times it felt a bit silly, but those rules kept us all alive. My parents were strict, but they had to be with so many of us.

There were plenty of "no's", but that opened the door for even more "yes's". The beauty is that we didn't see their rules as stern, mean-spirited punishments.

The marvelous part is that it worked. They set a high threshold and expected us to obey without questions or conditions – simply because they were our parents, and we were their children.

Through obedience, we experienced their love for us. Though we may not have liked rules at the time, especially during tough teenage years, we had a deep sense that they were all rooted in love. In fact, as a fence around a playground, rules actually gave us freedom to be ourselves and enjoy life within those boundaries.

Our relationship with God is designed much the same way. He expects us to obey Him at all times – unconditionally. It's not because God is a mean stick in the mud. He wants us to enjoy life within His boundaries – starting with the Ten Commandments.

4ᵗʰ Step to No Regrets: *Obey God Unconditionally.*

To fully live a life of no regrets, obey God no matter what – unconditionally – even when you don't feel like it.

Plain and simple, God wants us to do *what* we're told, *when* we're told, *because* we're told – without question or conditions. He made us. He knows what works. The Creator knows what's best for us. He makes the rules – not us.

We know what God expects us to do. It's all spelled out clearly in the Bible. We are to do *what* we're told. To know it, we have to read it. That's why it is so vital to know God and read His Holy Word every day.

Once we read it and know it, then work it. Saint James admonishes us, *"Do not merely listen to the word... Do what it says."* (James 1:22 NIV)

We are also to obey *when* we're told – immediately.

"Delayed obedience is disobedience."

My dear friend, Dr. Ron Kenoly, passed along these profound words. As a youngster growing up in Coffeyville, Kansas, his mother asked him to hang up the laundry while she went away one day. He decided instead to play ball with his buddies first and obey his mother later. When she returned home and found the wet laundry still wadded up in the clothes basket, the look of disappointment on her face and the words of her mouth ingrained an indelible impression on Ron.

"But, Mom, I had every intention of hanging up those clothes."

"Son, hell is full of people with good intentions. Delayed obedience is disobedience."

If God tells you to do something, don't put it off. Obey Him right away.

Abraham exemplified immediate and unconditional obedience in two amazing ways. When God first called him, God said, *"Leave your country, your relatives, and your father's house, and go to the land that I will show you. I will cause you to become the father of a great nation."* (Genesis 12:1-2) Abraham didn't question God or put up a fuss about having to leave everything and everyone behind. He obeyed God unconditionally – without even a clue about where he was going! God just told him to go and wait for directions later.

Many years later, long after Isaac's birth, God asked Abraham to sacrifice his only son back to the Lord. Abraham never once hesitated. In fact, *"The next morning Abraham got up early."* (Genesis 22:3) I don't know if I could have done that: willingly wake up early to go sacrifice my son. I might have slept in or waited a week or a month to fast, pray, and ponder God's bizarre command. Because of Abraham's faith and unconditional obedience, he was *"called 'the friend of God.'"* (James 2:23)

Besides doing *what* God tells us *when* He tells us, we must also obey God simply *because* He tells us – because He is God. He is the Potter, and we are the clay.

It's not for the clay to question or second-guess the Potter. We didn't make Him. He made us.

As parents, it often feels as though the first years of our children's lives are dominated by the word, "No." Our aim is to teach our children to obey. That takes time and a lot of correction.

It's similar between God and us. God's Word is full of plenty of "No's", but it is filled with even more "Yes's".

As a parent, I constantly stressed the importance of obeying. After Nicholas slipped up, I'd sit down with him, look him square in the eyes and ask, "Nicholas, how do you obey?"

"Quickly and quietly."

"Very good. And, when do you obey?"

"The first time."

"Thank you, my son. I love you."

That routine took a lot of repetition to sink in. Eventually, he got it.

God's rules serve two distinct functions: to protect us and to provide for us.

When my parents told me to wear my lifejacket, they wanted to protect me. When God says, "Thou shall not kill," He wants to protect us and others from the perils of evil.

When God, my parents, and the Church instruct me not to have sexual intercourse before marriage, it's to protect me from all the possible consequences: premarital pregnancies, incurable diseases, fear, anxiety, and so on. These commands also serve to provide for me – to offer the pure and peaceful conditions for a blissful honeymoon, a passionate marriage, and a mind free of worry and unwanted flashbacks.

All through the Old Testament, the Israelites were in the biggest trouble with God when they didn't do what He said – when they didn't obey. My father often remarked, "I think God cusses." Well, at one point, out of sheer frustration with the Israelites, God finally said, *"All right. This is the covenant I am going to make with you. I will perform wonders that have never been done before anywhere in all the earth or in any nation. ...Your responsibility is to obey all the commands I am giving you today."* (Exodus 34:10-11)

God's rules are very simple. All He asks us to do is obey.

That's why it is so vitally important for parents to teach their children to obey. It establishes the pattern by which we will respond to God. We become a slave to whatever we obey in life, to whatever controls us: an addiction, a habit, a hobby, a job, even a personal electronic device.

That's why I desire to know God and be a slave to Jesus Christ alone. *"Don't you realize that whatever you choose to obey becomes your master? You can choose sin, which leads to death, or you can choose to obey God and receive His approval."* (Romans 6:16)

The Blessed Mother obeyed God immediately when the angel, Gabriel, came to deliver the news. *"'I am the Lord's servant,' said Mary; 'may it happen to me as you have said.'"* (Luke 1:38 GNT)

Jesus obeyed His Blessed Mother at the wedding feast in Cana when He turned water into wine. He was obedient to His Father unconditionally, to the point of death. *"But even though he was God's Son, he learned through his sufferings to be obedient."* (Hebrews 5:8 GNT)

Early in my marriage with Melissa, we were still learning to trust God absolutely and obey Him unconditionally. We gave Him about 90% control, but we still kept that pesky 10% to ourselves that we didn't want to surrender to God. For the first three years of our marriage, I'm penitent to admit that we used contraceptives. We pushed God off the throne and assumed control ourselves. At the time, I didn't think much of it because I was a college graduate, newly married, living in California, and focused mainly on ourselves. Life was all about us. However, I violated God's laws and the Church's teachings on natural family planning.

I didn't obey God unconditionally. We understandably wanted to focus more on each other after our wedding day. There's nothing wrong with that, unless we bump God out of the picture in the process. We also knew the significant expense of raising a child in California. In our limited minds, we wanted to get out of debt before having children. There's nothing wrong with that either, except that we should have obeyed God unconditionally in 100% of our finances, intimate life, and our family.

God is so much bigger than what my mind can calculate or imagine. If I absolutely trust Him and unconditionally obey Him, then I can be confident God will grace us with children at the right time and provide everything we need to raise them.

I repented and asked God's forgiveness. We stopped playing God. We let God be God. After Makenah's birth in 1995, Melissa and I ceased contraception. Inga and I don't use it either. Our desire as a family is to obey God unconditionally – in the privacy of our bedroom, in the dollars of our checkbook, and in the work of our hands.

To say "Yes" to God, we have to say "No" to sin. After the flash flood, amidst my grief and tears, I could have easily obeyed addictions and allowed them to control me. Because my parents took the time to teach me early in life, I chose to obey God instead. I wanted God's approval. So, I said "Yes" to Him and "No" to sin.

I had to actively *"...take captive every thought to make it obedient to Christ."* (2 Corinthians 10:5 NIV) I chose to submit every temptation, unction, and notion to the confines of God's rules. What would God think? What does His Word say? What would my heavenly family think?

Thankfully, my obedience amidst adversity honored God and my heavenly family. As a result, He has blessed me beyond what I could have imagined with peace, joy, fulfillment, and a new life with my wife, Inga.

When King Saul was about to wage war, God gave him very specific and strict instructions to guarantee victory. All Saul had to do was obey them. Instead, he did things his way, much as the song goes, "*I did it my way.*" God was so appalled with King Saul, that He rejected him as king and established David as the new king. God Himself said, *"I greatly regret that I ever made Saul king, for he has not been loyal to me and has again refused to obey me."* (1 Samuel 15:11 NLT & NKJV) That's big regrets!

Samuel rebuked King Saul scolding, *"Why then did you not obey the voice of the Lord?"* (1 Samuel 15:19 NKJV) Saul tried to defend his actions retorting, *"But I did obey the Lord."* (1 Samuel 15:20) The problem was that Saul didn't fully obey God unconditionally. He cherry-picked a few commands and skipped the ones that weren't convenient.

Sound familiar? Sometimes we just prefer to pick a few commandments and brag about the ones we follow. We can't only obey convenient commandments. We must obey them all. He's not Lord *at* all if He's not Lord *of* all. We must obey God 100% unconditionally. Saint James declared, *"Whoever breaks one commandment is guilty of breaking them all."* (James 2:10 GNT)

God puts such a high premium on unconditional obedience that Samuel further reprimanded King Saul saying, *"What is more pleasing to the Lord: your burnt offerings and sacrifices or your obedience to his voice? Obedience is far better than sacrifice."* (1 Samuel 15:22) Wise King Solomon said it similarly. *"The Lord is more pleased when we do what is just and right than when we give him sacrifices."* (Proverbs 21:3)

Do you unconditionally obey God 100% in every area and aspect of your life? Ask the Holy Spirit, *"Search me, O God, and know my heart… Point out anything in me that offends you."* (Psalm 139:23-24)

Do you obey 90% of God's Commandments and ignore those other bothersome 10%? Let's revisit all Ten Commandments together and take a personal inventory.

(1) Have I put God first in all things, or has my work, hobby, or electronic device become an idol?

(2) Do I misuse God's Name flippantly throughout the day without even realizing it? The Bible

says that the *"Lord will not let you go unpunished if you misuse his name."* (Exodus 20:7) Father Larry Richards once challenged me to break old habits and only use God's Name with complete reverence. Since then, I've disciplined myself to avoid saying things such as, "Oh, my God" or "Oh, God," even though we mutter them innocently out of habit. It's disrespectful to Him.

(3) Have I kept the Lord's Day holy?

(4) Do I still honor my parents, even if they are divorced or deceased? My father, when faced with a precarious situation, was always guided by the thought, "What would my mother think?" Have I forgiven my parent or released any grudges I'm holding against them? When was the last time I told them that I love them? You may never get another chance.

(5) Have I had an abortion, or prevented life by using contraception? Perhaps I haven't murdered, but have I used hurtful or hateful words? The Bible says that *"the tongue can kill or nourish life."* (Proverbs 18:21) Our words are powerful and can harm or heal. Guard them carefully. Jesus plainly stated, *"...if you are angry with someone, you are subject to judgment! ...Come to terms quickly with your enemy before it is too late."* (Matthew 5:22, 25)

(6) Have I committed adultery? Perhaps I haven't cheated on my spouse outright, but have I fantasized about it? Jesus said, *"...anyone who even looks at a woman with lust in his eye has already committed adultery with her in his heart."* (Matthew 5:28) If a lustful thought has taken root in my heart, then I'm already guilty of committing the sin. *"For as he thinks in his heart, so is he."* (Proverbs 23:7 NKJV)

(7-10) Have I stolen, lied, or coveted anyone or anything that isn't mine?

I realize this litany of provoking questions can be convicting and difficult. If you feel guilty or convicted reading these, then thank God for that unction from His Holy Spirit. Thank God that through His mercy, He doesn't give us the punishment we deserve. Thank God that Jesus stayed bound to the cross to set you free – so that you don't have to be bound to guilt and sin. Even if you've had an abortion or something you regret terribly, bring it before Jesus now and put the past in His Hands as you ask His forgiveness. Ask your baby in Heaven – by name – to forgive you.

Thank God that we have this moment right now to reconcile the past, repent, and start living a life of no regrets. To obey God unconditionally, we need to begin with His Ten Commandments.

So, how about that inconvenient Third Commandment? Do I avoid work and really rest on the Sabbath? Hasn't that one become passé and completely optional this day and age – particularly when work is ever-present before our eyes with smartphones, emails, and electronic devices?

I understand how tough this one is. Life is so incredibly active, and we often have a huge list of chores for the weekend, many of which tend to spill over into Sunday. Perhaps it's a big week ahead, and we want to get an early start Sunday on emails or office-work to be primed and ready for Monday.

I constantly challenge myself to rest. Relax after church, for it is a *"day of rest dedicated to the Lord your God. On that day no one in your household may do any kind of work."* (Exodus 20:10) Spend time with your family with no other agenda than to be together and make memories.

Avoid the temptation to squeeze in a few chores or emails.

God has *"blessed the Sabbath day and set it apart as holy."* (Exodus 20:11) God's time and your family time should not be for sale. How can I possibly be so audacious to presume that if I don't finish a bit of extra work on Sunday, then the world might stop spinning on Monday – or God might stop providing my family's needs?

God is our Provider. Let God be God. Just do what He says. Leave the rest up to Him. He is faithful to fulfill His promises.

The One who made us knows how we tick. If *"God rested from all his work"* (Genesis 2:2) after creating everything in six days, and if we are made in His image (Genesis 1:26), then how much more do we need a full day of rest after six days of work and daily duties? The Creator knows what our bodies, minds, and families need. Simply obey Him in this, and He promises to work out the rest.

Obeying God in this area of rest helped me tremendously to heal after my family died. During rest, our bodies heal and our minds unwind, sorting through endless details of the day. I believe that God also ministers to our soul and spirits – when we take the time to rest and be still.

Psalm 23 illustrates this beautifully. As I *"lie down in green pastures,"* God *"restores my soul."* (Psalm 23:2-3 NIV) I experienced this firsthand after the flash flood. As I took time to rest, God gradually healed me. Thankfully and miraculously, I had very few nightmares or unsettling dreams. Somehow, my sleep was deep. I can only attribute it to the goodness of God. I'm fully convinced that He used deep sleep to perform deep surgery on my soul and restore it bit by bit, night after night.

If you're still recovering from a situation or going through a valley, I encourage you to especially obey God in the area of the Third Commandment. Take time to rest in God's presence.

"Be still, and know that I am God." (Psalm 46:10 NIV)

Let Him lead you by those still waters and restore your soul. If you have difficulty sleeping, pray and read a Psalm before you lie down. Ask God to minister unto you, that your sleep might be deep and sweet. (Psalm 4:8, Proverbs 3:24, Jeremiah 31:25-26)

Chapter Eight

New Life

> *"...obey the Lord and keep all the commands I am giving you today. The Lord your God will make you successful in everything you do. He will give you many children and numerous livestock, and your fields will produce abundant harvests, for the Lord will delight in being good to you... The Lord your God will delight in you if you obey his voice and keep the commands and laws written in this Book of the Law, and if you turn to the Lord your God with all your heart and soul."* (Deuteronomy 30:8-10)

The winter after Inga and I married, we were graciously offered a free retreat at a cabin high in the Rockies west of Colorado Springs. One evening in the cabin with a fire blazing in the fireplace and ravioli warming on the gas stove, Inga handed me a present as we sat on the sofa.

I untied the ribbon, lifted the lid, and carefully pulled back the tissue paper. To my astonishment, I uncovered two bibs, one pink and one blue. Each said, "I love my daddy."

In shocked amazement, my eyes danced from the pink bib to the blue bib and back.

"We're going to have a baby?"

"Yes, my darling!!"

Through the ashes of my past, God was bringing forth new life. I was completely speechless. My heart leapt for joy. I was going to be a daddy again!

The remainder of the pregnancy was tenuous due to a toxemia diagnosis. With multiple ultrasounds and fetal stress tests, we were on pins and needles for many months.

On Friday, July 27th at about 3:30 in the morning, we headed to the hospital. After 14 hours of intense labor, Inga was weary as 6:00 P.M. approached.

Given the day's lack of progress and Inga's still tenuous toxemia blood levels, her doctor highly recommended a C-Section for the safety of Inga and our baby.

I so much wanted this day to go differently. I thought I had trusted and obeyed God enough that He would bless us with an uncomplicated labor, perfect delivery, and happy baby.

Sometimes, even with all we've been through, life still happens. We're not in Heaven yet. Complications still arise. People still die. We live in an imperfect world, and things don't always turn out as we plan.

I still had to trust God's plan – even though I didn't understand. I've lived a lot of life and death already. I've learned to trust God a great deal. Still, my faith was tested and stretched even further.

God is still on the throne. He has the last word. I had to continue to obey God unconditionally and stay in faith, not in fear.

They began the C-Section surgery and before we knew it, they lifted up a perfectly healthy baby.

"It's a…boy!" I exclaimed with pure joy.

"We have a son!"

Tears of thanksgiving filled my eyes as I made my way to the warming table. They swaddled him and placed him in my arms. There in the operating room at Inga's side, I serenaded our son with a lullaby I recently composed.

Once I received the go-ahead, I high-stepped it as fast as my legs would take me to announce the news to everyone in the waiting room.

As the double doors burst forth, so did my joy and my resounding words.

"We have a son!"

From our huddles of despair in 2003 at the flood-site and graveside years ago – where we had embraced one another and clung to each other's arms for dear life – to this moment now of elation in 2007, a flood of tears gushed forth out of absolute relief and thanksgiving to Almighty God for His goodness.

We named him Ezekiel Thomas, meaning, "a divinely blessed and preserved warrior with the strength of God." I'll never forget the drive home in the stillness of that balmy summer night: three miracles in one car.

Once inside, all I could do was kneel and wail as I embraced Ezekiel tightly to my chest. My stomach cringed in convulsions of crying – much as in the past – but this time from tears of joy and thanksgiving.

Words were no longer adequate. This moment loudly proclaimed the goodness of God's grace, His blessings through brokenness, and abundant beauty from ashes. It was as though God was bellowing through the walls, *"I have come in order that you might have life – life in all its fullness."* (John 10:10 GNT)

About eight months later, Inga was feeling a bit queasy over the smell of yogurt and vinegar. We both watched with anticipation as the pregnancy test slowly illuminated a big "+" sign. We were expecting again!

It felt as though our unconditional obedience to God led Him to fill our joy to overflowing.

Thankfully, this pregnancy was comparatively uneventful. December arrived and we went strolling through the mall. At the top of an escalator, Inga suddenly buckled in pain from a contraction.

After a long, sleepless night of resting, walking, and contracting, we headed to the hospital at 4:00 in the morning. After a few hours of monitoring contractions, Inga's nurse and doctor noticed something strangely odd and extremely rare that prevented dilation and normal delivery. Our baby couldn't get through. She immediately prepped for another C-Section.

As I waited alone outside the surgery room again, I shared a few choice words with God. Why? Why was it so difficult for our children to enter this world – every single one of them?

Once I vented my frustrations, I faced the prospect that God must tremendously trust us to allow us to traverse through so many trials. Life is not always fair, but God is always good. He must have a mighty mission for our family – to stretch our faith and obedience so relentlessly.

Within a few minutes, I was once again holding Inga's hand beside her in the operating room. Moments later the doctor lifted up our beautifully formed baby.

"It's a…girl! We have a daughter!"

She looked stunning – perfectly formed in every way. At 9:57 A.M. on Sunday December 7th, 2008, we gave birth to our first little girl: Estellah Eve, meaning, "a star and a highly esteemed woman full of life."

It is evident – even through our children's difficult births – that obeying God unconditionally enables us to live a life of no regrets. Had I not obeyed God for years leading up to now – even when obedience was the more difficult choice – I'm convinced we wouldn't have experienced these incredible blessings now.

Simple unconditional obedience to God – as it does with parents – speaks volumes and goes a long way. Just as Abraham obeyed God unconditionally and surrendered his beloved son, God blessed him abundantly. *"This is what the Lord says: Because you have obeyed me… I will bless you richly. …and through your descendants, all the nations of the earth will be blessed – all because you have obeyed me."* (Genesis 22:16-18)

Long before the flood and still now, years later, my prayer every morning is this:

"Lord, I'm willing and available to be obedient to You."

It's a simple prayer. It surrenders my heart, my will, and my life to God – through unconditional obedience.

Similar to the prayers of the prophets, another of my regular daily prayers to God is, *"Here I am, Lord. Your servant is listening. I come to do your will."*

It's unconditional obedience in action.

I have the sense that unconditional obedience brings a smile to God's face – as a parent feels when children obey. When we obey God, His delight gives us strength and peace. His joy gives us joy. In fact, Jesus declared, *"When you obey me, you remain in my love, just as I obey my Father and remain in his love. I have told you this so that you will be filled with my joy. Yes, your joy will overflow!"* (John 15:10-11) A life overflowing with joy is indeed a life of no regrets!

Do you want joy?

Obeying God unconditionally is how.

God Himself said that *"…I lavish my love on those who love me and obey my commands, even for a thousand generations."* (Exodus 20:6)

Just as my parents delighted in me and lavished their love on me as I obeyed them, so does God. In fact,

God not only delights in those who fully obey Him, but He restores. (Deuteronomy 30:3) He bestows bountiful blessings (Deuteronomy 28:1-13), and He gives success, offspring, and abundance to those who simply obey. (Deuteronomy 30:8-10)

If you wish to live a life of no regrets, then obey God unconditionally – even when you are tempted, tried, and tested. Obey Him amidst your adversity. It's worth the blessings, honor, and grace God will grant in return.

As my parents delighted in me when I did *what* I was told, *when* I was told, *because* I was told, so will God.

To be a friend of God as Abraham and Moses were, obey Him as they did. Jesus said, *"You are my friends if you obey me."* (John 15:14)

To experience indescribable joy and peace as God's very friend, discipline yourself to obey God unconditionally as you journey toward a life of no regrets.

Step 4 Action Points

1) Make a no-regrets decision to *Obey God Unconditionally.*

2) Make a daily discipline to obey God immediately. "Delayed obedience is disobedience."

3) Make Godly obedience a lifestyle by obeying your parents (regardless of your age) and teaching your children to obey.

Step 5
Chapter Nine

Love is Sacrifice

> *"Husbands, love your wives just as Christ loved the church and gave his life for it. Men ought to love their wives just as they love their own bodies. ...every husband must love his wife as himself, and every wife must respect her husband."* (Ephesians 5:25, 28, 33 GNT)

"If mamma's not happy, nobody's going to be happy."

How true it is. I don't know who first invented that phrase, but songs have been written about it and the principle is right on. If the matriarch of the family isn't happy, then pretty much nobody in the household is bound to be happy. Conversely, if she is happy, at least everyone else has the chance to be happy.

As a kind Amish gentleman once said to me, "A happy wife: a happy life!"

"Yes, Dear."

I often heard my father swallow his pride, bite his tongue, and say those words regularly to my mother, Mary Frances. If she preferred to turn left, he just said, "Yes,

Francie" and steered the car left. If she craved Chick-fil-A even though he would rather eat at home, he just said, "Yes, Dear" and aimed the car for the restaurant.

It doesn't mean that Dad was a weak follower by any means. On the contrary, he was the strongest man and leader I've ever known. He led quietly, through example and as a servant to others.

He didn't cave in to her out of weakness. He wasn't a pansy who yielded to her every whim. Rather, when my father honored my mother, it was always a sacrificial act of strength. Surrender in this sense is not weakness as so many presume. It's an act of valor.

The founder of the Salvation Army, William Booth, put it this way. *"The greatness of a man's power is in the measure of his surrender."*

Surrender gives way to victory. When we surrender our lives to God, then He can live victoriously through us.

Christ is the ultimate example. He surrendered every moment to His Father, including His victorious final breath, *"Father! In your hands I place my spirit!"* (Luke 23:46 GNT) Jesus made Himself nothing, took on the very *"nature of a servant,"* and was obedient to death on a cross. (Philippians 2:7-8)

Jesus proclaimed, *"…whoever humbles himself will be made great."* (Matthew 23:12 GNT) Furthermore, *"If one of you wants to be great, you must be the servant of the rest; and if one of you wants to be first, you must be the slave of the others like the Son of Man, who did not come to be served, but to serve and to give his life…"* (Matthew 20:26-28 GNT)

Are you willing to serve, sacrifice, and surrender? Are you willing to set aside your own stature to elevate those around you? It displays tremendous strength, confidence, and content about your character. It means that you are unwavering in who you are as a person. I've heard it said that the true measure of yourself is not how many people serve you, but how many people you serve.

In other words, the best way to build yourself up is to lay your life down. Jesus taught us how. He decreed, *"love one another, just as I love you. The greatest love you can have...is to give your life..."* (John 15:12-13 GNT)

5th Step to No Regrets: *Serve Your Spouse Sacrificially.*

Whether you're a husband or wife, single or celibate, we can all glean much from this step. Just because priests, nuns, or other clergy aren't married doesn't mean they don't have a spouse. Their spouse is the Church, for which they've given up their lives – serving sacrificially.

If you are single and desire to marry one day, sacrifice your life from now on for your future spouse by staying chaste. Serve others sacrificially with these precepts to prepare for your mate. For now, *"Your Creator will be like a husband to you - the Lord Almighty is his name."* (Isaiah 54:5 GNT) Maintain your purity and learn to serve God sacrificially as a spouse. You'll be better prepared for the love it takes for a marriage to flourish.

The first three Commandments address our relationship with God, as do the first four *Steps to No Regrets*. It has to begin with God and flow outward to everyone else.

God patterned marriage after His relationship with us. It's a parallel image of God's love for us. So, if we can get our relationship right with God, then we are equipped for a no-regrets relationship with our spouse.

My father loved my mother enough to lay down his own wishes and "die" to his own desires in order to honor and serve her. Likewise, I also heard Mom frequently say things such as, "I should have listened to your father. He was right and so wise." She respected him publically and privately more than we knew. She cherished his wisdom and courage.

Together, they demonstrated a beautiful circle of love and respect. After more than 60 years of successful marriage, they knew a bit about what it took. Evidently, it worked.

"And you husbands must love your wives with the same love Christ showed the church. He gave up his life for her to make her holy and clean, washed by baptism and God's word. …So again I say, each man must love his wife… and the wife must respect her husband." (Ephesians 5:25-26, 33)

As a husband, I am commanded to love my wife as Christ loves the church. That's not a suggestion. Christ came to serve, and then died for us. *"Go and do likewise."* (Luke 10:37 NIV) So, according to Jesus, I'm to do the same. *"I have given you an example to follow. Do as I have done to you."* (John 13:15)

In other words, my life for myself is over.

That is okay.

My wife is worth my life. I'm here to serve her.

Take the initiative to love and serve your spouse. Don't merely model love. Become Christ crucified. Partake of it, and be Christ to your spouse.

Jesus declared more than once that when we lose our life, we find it. (Matthew 10:39, Matthew 16:25, Luke 17:33, John 12:25) Jesus considered us worth His life when He hung on the cross for us. When Jesus sacrificed His life, God redeemed His as well as ours. The paradox is that when we give up our life, we actually gain true life.

My father epitomized this rule of thumb: *"Son, just do what your wife asks."* It may cost a little extra time or a little more money, but it will save a lot more time and aggravation in the long run. It will make life a lot simpler and marriage a lot smoother.

I enlist my father's wisdom in my marriage all the time. Inga rarely does anything just for herself. She respects me beyond measure in public and in private. She somehow respects my past, my heavenly family, and this ministry of sharing our story repeatedly. She has formidable faith and relentless respect. On top of that, I don't think I've ever heard her complain or ask for anything (except for more shoes).

Occasionally, around Christmas time, if she wishes to go shopping, my response is no longer filled with grumbling or complaining. I've learned to say, "Yes, Dear. How long would you like to shop? Would you like me to come along with you or stay home with our children?"

It's not about being "henpecked" or bossed-around. It's about sacrificial service. You'd be amazed at the dividends this sacrificial attitude of servant-hood yields in our relationship.

I don't say "Yes, Dear" in a fake, facetious, or sarcastic tone, but with sincere gladness in my heart. Just as I do my best to *"Serve the Lord with gladness,"* (Psalm 100:2 NKJV) I endeavor to maintain that same attitude as I serve my spouse. I still miss it and mess up plenty of times. My intent is to never let my spouse out-serve me. I strive to serve her constantly.

After nearly twelve years of marriage to Melissa, and well over seven to Inga, I've learned two words that have really helped make life a lot easier.

Give up.

That's right, give up.

No, don't give up on your marriage. Give up yourself as Christ *"gave up his life for her."* (Ephesians 5:25) I realize this notion bucks against every fiber of our being and our culture. We don't like to lose, surrender, or appear weak. After all, what would our friends say? Well, you're the one who has to live under the same roof together. If you want happiness and tranquility in your home, give up. Serve sacrificially.

When a man serves his wife with the same sacrifice as Christ – laying down his life – he will truly discover the dynamics of a no-regrets marriage as God intended. That couple will uncover a whole new dimension of love, romance, and intimacy as never before.

The majority of the Ephesians Scripture is directed towards men. Evidently Saint Paul figured us guys needed two thumps on the head – to drill the message deep enough past our skull to penetrate our minds and hearts. He was right to repeat. Twice he commands imperatively that the man *"must love"* his wife.

Rarely does it come easily or naturally for most men. We often have to work at it.

Curiously, Paul never gives women the same edict. He emphasizes another dynamic of the marriage relationship: respect. *"The wife must respect her husband."* Again the word *"must"* is used – perhaps because respect is as vital to men as sacrificial love is to women. (Dr. Emerson Eggerichs wrote extensively about this in an excellent book entitled, *"Love & Respect"* [Thomas Nelson, 2004]).

Respecting men must be very challenging – often because we don't deserve it. Respecting a selfish man who doesn't adore God or esteem his wife must be immensely difficult. Yet, even when we don't adore God, He still loves us unconditionally. He gives us goodness we don't deserve, such as everlasting life, mercy, and forgiveness. That's grace. Men seem to thrive on unconditional respect as much as women thrive on unconditional love. One will activate the other.

Years ago, when I finally completed a big work project with a significant engineering customer, the bottom fell out when a competitor waltzed away with 100% of the business. All my effort, energy, and expectations were completely dashed. I was disheartened. Melissa displayed her respect for me through a simple note on a scrap of paper.

> *"My love – …Don't be discouraged and remember He is still in control even when things aren't fair. …God knows what He is doing. You know all of this. I am always proud to be your wife…more each day…I love you & I believe in you. Faithfully yours, Melissa"*

Her words of respect infused me with courage and let me know that I still had what it takes. I went back to work with a new spring in my step and a deeper sacrificial love for my wife.

Too many marriages and relationships suffer regrets from broken promises and selfish motives. They are based on "What are you doing for me?" and function as "outside-in" – consuming, rather than giving.

The marriage relationship is a reflection of the Gospel. The man must unconditionally serve his wife with complete sacrifice, as Christ died for the Church. The woman must unconditionally respect her undeserved husband, as God does through unmerited grace.

Both of these assignments take enormous sacrifice.

Love is sacrifice.

To give yourself up, to serve, respect, and love – all take supreme sacrifice. As Jesus displayed it on the cross, so we are to serve our spouses and give up our lives.

After our third wedding anniversary in 2009, I had to rush Inga to the hospital when her seat cushion was suddenly covered in blood. We had no idea what was happening. They stabilized her with some pain meds and an I-V. Then a lab tech took us down the hall for an ultrasound.

In the quietness of the dimly lit room during the procedure, he barely said two words. From what I could gather on the screen it looked as if there was a baby inside. It didn't appear to be moving, nor did I see or hear a heartbeat.

"Please, Lord. Not again. Not to Inga."

I fervently muttered prayers to God, pleading with Him for life.

The blood report came back and confirmed what we now suspected: Inga was pregnant. They concluded that her body was probably trying to naturally abort our deceased child. I didn't want to believe it.

Within a few minutes, they prepped for surgery and gave me a beeper to alert me when they finished. I walked aimlessly in the parking lot and prayed earnestly under the soothing September sun. I wandered into the hospital chapel and knelt down to pray and read Scripture.

I tearfully flashed back six years ago to the hospital chapel in Emporia, Kansas, when I knelt in similar fashion after identifying all four of my children's bodies. There, I uttered a prayer of simple trust to God amidst unconscionable questions.

So, here on September 15th, 2009, I once again committed our lives – my wife and unborn child – to God. "Into Your hands, Lord, I place our trust. Into Your hands, Lord, I place my family."

Suddenly, the beeper buzzed, blinked, and startled me in the middle of my prayer. I rushed out to the waiting area and was directed to a post-op room to meet with her doctor.

"Inga's stable. She lost a lot of blood."

Evidently she required four transfusions and four layers of stitches. Her doctor continued.

"And, I didn't find what I was expecting."

My heart braced for the worst, but hoped for the best as I hung on every word. She pulled out an 8" by 10" photo just taken of our baby – our deceased child – the one they just delivered – a beautiful boy.

"I'm so sorry, Robert."

I welled up with tears and thanked the doctor for everything.

I was left alone in the small stark consultation room as I just stared at our son. He was five inches long, completely intact, and perfectly formed – fingers, toes, arms, legs, head, mouth, eyes, and nose. It was unfathomable. Now I had seven children in Heaven. I cried and prayed aloud.

"Lord, why? Not again. Not with Inga. I don't want her to face death this way and have to bury a child, too."

My mind raced for reasons. What was God up to now? Hadn't I been through enough already? Couldn't He spare Inga from such pain?

Nevertheless, we won't abandon our faith. We won't stop trusting God – even now. He won't abandon us.

I hurried upstairs and found Inga in the ICU.

We both gazed upon our son's picture and sobbed together.

Amidst all the nurses coming and going, one slowly entered reverently cradling a small blanket.

"I thought you might like to see your son."

My heart hit the floor. There lying on the blanket was our little son – all five inches of him – perfectly formed.

She gently placed him into my hands and left the room. Inga and I just gazed upon his frail but beautiful frame. We touched him and wept openly as questions inundated my mind.

Why? Why, God? Why us?

This moment was uniquely overwhelming.

Joining hands, Inga and I offered him up to God together saying, "Lord, into your hands we commend his spirit." We sang "Jesus Loves Me" as our voices cracked and lingered with the lyrics, "Little ones to Him belong."

We kissed him goodnight and continued grieving with hope for the day when we would see him again. For now, he carried a piece of our hearts to Heaven.

We named our son, "little Dale" – after Inga's grandfather – and buried him a few days later at the cemetery. We placed orange lilies alongside his tiny white coffin and sang "It Is Well with My Soul" as we released an orange balloon to Heaven for him.

Love is all about sacrifice. I learned an even greater depth of loving Inga during that dreadful time. We grew closer to God and to one another as we clung to our faith and hoped for more children.

It's in sacrificial giving that we truly receive – the peace of a fulfilling relationship – the way God designed and demonstrated it. It means going all out and loving one another with no regrets from the inside-out.

It's all about, "How can I best serve you?"

Chapter Ten

Fall in Love with Jesus

> *"This is my body, which is given for you. Do this in remembrance of me."* (1 Corinthians 11:24)

My dear friends, Cheryl and Dan, demonstrate sacrificial love beautifully. Cheryl has an engineering degree and assists Dan with his business. Some time ago, Cheryl suffered severe headaches. Soon after, a brain aneurism burst. The doctors effectively deemed her brain inactive and her life to be over. Dan and their children believed otherwise.

With heaps of prayers and pounds of perseverance, they never gave up on Cheryl. They stayed by her hospital bedside when her body couldn't move and her mouth couldn't speak or eat. When all she could do was blink, I witnessed firsthand the bottomless depth of love through their eyes as Dan held her hand, gave up his life for his wife daily – with no promise of anything in return, and communicated with relentless determination a sacrificial love louder than mere words. They both emanated a sparkle like two teenagers in love. They peered deeply within each other as if to say, "I still adore you. I believe in you. I'm not giving up."

Miracle after miracle, therapy after therapy, and surgery after surgery, Cheryl gradually began to regain her cognitive and physical abilities. Today, she talks and moves more slowly than before, but her whit is still sharp as a tack. Cheryl may no longer be the same woman Dan married, but he pledged to sacrificially serve her through better or worse. This was some of the worse. Now, their love has been purified as gold through fire (1 Peter 1:7) and is more passionate than ever before.

That's a no-regrets marriage. How many men would have jumped ship, pulled the plug, or just given up on their wives? Instead, Dan gave himself up for his wife. His wife is worth his life. Now, God has blessed them beyond comprehension.

To live a life of no regrets, proactively nurture, cherish, and nourish one another with words of affirmation. It takes concerted effort for both spouses to suppress negative thoughts and release the positive ones.

My parents never stopped urging us eight children to speak kindly and maintain harmony with one another and our spouses. Words go a long way. The tongue can heal or hurt. (Proverbs 18:21) I find I still must intentionally choose words to build up, not tear down.

Guard your words. Once you utter them, you can never take them back. Similar to toothpaste out of the tube, no matter how hard you try, you can never squeeze them back. People forgive, but they don't soon forget that hurtful tone or painful word. Try your best to speak respectfully with one another, being very careful of your tone of voice. Those little nuances matter. Little things are big things.

Savor your spouse and affirm frequently how lovely or attractive they look. Adorn your spouse with words of affection, affirmation, and adoration. As you do, you'll find that they will become more attractive day by day. I witnessed this firsthand. Many attest to the fact that Melissa and Inga each became even more beautiful as the years went by.

I'm fully convinced that the way your spouse looks is a direct reflection of the way you treat one another. If you're concerned about their appearance in the mirror, be sure to examine the reflection of your treatment first.

In fact, the way a man treats his wife not only impacts her appearance, but it also affects the way God answers his prayers. Saint Peter emphasized, *"...you husbands must give honor to your wives. ...she is your equal partner in God's gift of new life. If you don't treat her as you should, your prayers will not be heard."* (1 Peter 3:7) Whoa.

That verse slams me between the eyes. In other words, if it feels as if your prayers are falling on deaf ears, it's time to take inventory of your love life. How's your love life? How's your prayer life? How are you treating your wife? They are all closely intertwined.

Part of Saint Paul's instructions to husbands is also *"...to make her holy and clean, washed by baptism and God's word."* (Ephesians 5:26) Among other things, this infers that we should bathe her in God's Word. As priest of your home, read Scripture together. The very act of speaking sacred Scripture will cleanse, refresh, revive, and sanctify your marriage as you wash it daily with the water of God's Word.

One of the most romantic moments of the day can be in bed at nighttime snuggled together and reciting Scriptures from the Bible. Turn off the TV and turn on the Almighty Word of God. You'll be amazed at how it fortifies your faith as a couple and deepens your intimacy as you drift off to sleep.

I once heard a woman remark how there's nothing more attractive than a man on his knees in prayer. Inga has confessed to me that my strong faith is one of the things that first attracted her to me. A man's passion for God is an indication of his passion for his wife.

There's something about a person of deep faith that is attractive. I believe it is Jesus inside that becomes visible outside.

Fall in love with Jesus, and your spouse will fall in love with you.

When they see Jesus *in* you and *through* you, it can't help but draw them *to* you. We are all drawn towards our Creator through Jesus. When He indwells in you, your spouse will naturally gravitate towards God in you.

Be a person of prayer, passion, and devotion to Christ. Pray together daily as a couple and you will draw closer to each other as you draw nearer to God. Immerse yourself in the Word of God together. It will teach you how to serve your spouse sacrificially. Falling deeper in love with Jesus will do wonders to strengthen the strands of your marriage relationship. Intimacy with God will cultivate intimacy with your mate. The passion within your heart will ignite the passion within your spouse's heart. It will continually renew and rekindle your intimacy with one another.

Remain faithful to one another, in thoughts, words, and deeds. Don't cheat. Period. It's not worth it. Don't even entertain the thoughts. Don't talk about it. Don't do it. My parents never did. I never did. Your spouse is worth your undivided affection. If you have children, they deserve your faithful devotion that much more. Whether married, single, or celibate, *"If you keep yourself pure, you will be a utensil God can use for his purpose. Your life will be clean, and you will be ready for the Master to use you for every good work."* (2 Timothy 2:21)

One of my most gratifying no-regrets moments after the flash flood was declaring that I was faithful to Melissa and our children for all our years together: nearly twelve years of marriage and eight years as a father. As a travelling Field Applications Engineer, I had plenty of opportunities out of town when I could have cheated. I chose not to. My children proudly wore a T-Shirt I bought years ago that said, "My Daddy is a Promise Keeper!" I meant every word of it and abided by it. I still do. Our children are watching.

Avoid precarious situations to prevent yourself from cheating in the first place. Don't visit promiscuous internet websites. Don't stare at the provocative magazines in the checkout line. Your eyes are the windows to your soul. Don't let anything through those windows that might pollute your soul or your marriage. *"Run from anything that stimulates youthful lust. Follow anything that makes you want to do right."* (2 Timothy 2:22) Don't worship lust. Don't allow it to become a god. You cannot serve two masters. (Matthew 6:24, Luke 16:13)

Don't go anywhere near those "adult" book stores or so-called "gentlemen's clubs." If you're truly an adult gentleman, then deny your selfish desires, buy some flowers instead, and bring them home to your wife for some genuine lasting romance. Make your spouse the object of your affections. Next to God, let her be your consuming desire.

Face it. Pornography will never satisfy. It's an insatiable temptation that only grows more decadent and insidious the more you feed it. Instead, feed your marriage and starve the temptation.

Illicit flings – whether in mind or in body – will always lead to regrets. If you want a no-regrets life and a no-regrets marriage, I urge you to heed these words. God's commandments will protect your family and provide the fertile soil for a flourishing marriage.

If you've messed up and cheated on your spouse, then start your life of no-regrets together today. Clean the slate with each other. Begin anew. Forgive. Let God into your marriage to do a new thing. Establish in your heart that you will never regress to the regrets of the past. Declare it on a written piece of paper and have both of you sign and date it. Don't live in or dwell on the past. Extend miles of grace, mercy, and respect for each other. God can make all things new, heal your wounds, and gradually restore your souls.

Perhaps you feel the temptations drawing you away from your marriage are just too strong. "I just can't help myself," you might think. As my father often said, "Can't means won't." Combat every temptation as Jesus did in the desert. Begin with the words, *"It is written."* (Matthew 4:4, 7, 10 NIV) Quote the Sword of the Spirit – the Word of God. Say something such as this.

"I nail the passions and desires of my sinful nature to the cross and crucify them there." (Galatians 5:24 paraphrased)

Say it over and over until the temptation leaves you. Repeat the verse, *"I have the strength to face all conditions by the power that Christ gives me."* (Philippians 4:13 GNT)

Remember, *"...God is always at work in you to make you willing and able to obey his own purpose."* (Philippians 2:13 GNT) If you know God personally through Jesus Christ, you already have the power within you through the Holy Spirit to resist temptation, to *"stand up under it"* (1 Corinthians 10:13 NIV), and remain faithful to your spouse.

Lean into God and away from the temptation. Hop on the exercise bike or take a cold shower if you must. Deny yourself.

Serve your spouse sacrificially. Men, give up your life for your wife.

Guard the sanctity of your marriage at all costs. It is sacred. It's not just an agreement or a document. It's a sacrament and covenant. Don't cast your pearls before swine. The marital embrace is more than a handshake. God sees the two as becoming one.

Jesus said, *"This is my body, which is given for you. Do this in remembrance of me."* (1 Corinthians 11:24) In addition to its context of the Last Supper and Holy Communion, try letting Jesus' words challenge you from a deeper angle.

He gave up His body for you. Have you given up your body for your spouse? Have you done it in remembrance of Him?

Jesus' body was broken for you. Have you sacrificially broken your body of its desires and surrendered your flesh for your spouse? Do it in remembrance of what Jesus did for you.

Men, don't neglect your wife. Just because it's the day after your honeymoon, that doesn't mean you can ignore her. Don't suddenly check your wife off your list and kiss dating goodbye.

Do just the opposite. Step up your courting constantly for the rest of your marriage. Date, romance, and pursue her well after your wedding night. Keep mystique, intrigue, and romance alive within your marriage.

We all like to know that we're worth being fussed over and pursued. Show emotion, passion, and appreciation. Dream together and write them down. Pay your bills, figure your finances, and give your tithe together. If you do nothing as one, the two of you will drift apart as two canoes floating in a pond.

I found some simple yet powerful phrases that helped me immensely to live a no-regrets marriage. You might practice them right now by saying them out loud. Some are more difficult than others.

"I am sorry."

"I was wrong."

"Please forgive me."

"I love you."

"I'll ask for directions." (Especially for us men.)

Find reasons throughout the year to celebrate! Big anniversaries or simple first moments are all good reasons to share an ice cream, a meal, or a basket brimming with scrumptious fries. If your budget is tight, then be creative with your dates. You can do a lot with a buck at the dollar store. Dream up a treasure hunt, plan an adventure at a park, or just write a poem or a song.

When Inga and I lived in an apartment, I transformed the living room into a romantic candle-lit dining nook with a table cloth and a card table. I cooked dinner, chilled a cheap bottle of sparkling cider, and made a video from our pictures and an original composition. We made a priceless memory and celebrated our marriage for fewer than ten bucks.

Don't just kiss each other dutifully. Kiss with passion! Try it for seven seconds straight every morning and evening while placing your fingertips on each other's head. You'll never regret it.

Don't mutter a monotone "Okay, I Love You." routinely as your "goodbye" on the phone. Intentionally say, "I love you!" with enthusiasm. Chew, savor, and devour those three words. Don't assume that just because you bring home a paycheck, your spouse automatically knows your love. You must say it. After all, Jesus did. He demonstrated it to the fullest extent. He also affirmed the words, *"I love you."* (John 15:9 GNT)

Let your spouse perpetually be in the inner shrine of your thoughts. He is your king. She is your queen. Place him or her on the pedestal of your heart. Write short love notes. If you travel, send postcards while you're away or hide one that your spouse is sure to find after you leave. Always esteem and think more highly of your spouse than yourself. Complement one another and show appreciation for even seemingly mundane things.

It's natural to glean a good deal of self-esteem from your marriage relationship. If you nourish your relationship, you'll nourish your spouse. If you nourish your career, you'll starve your spouse. That may prompt him or her to wander elsewhere for a sense of significance.

Love your spouse as they prefer to be loved. Learn little things that please them. For example, Inga loves Valentine's Day to celebrate romance. So, I do it up and make a special fuss over her – similar to the time I first expressed that I loved her on Valentine's Day.

I also hold the door for her – nearly every time. It's a small courtesy to daily reinforce that she's more important. I give up my life for her.

Melissa never cared much for Valentine's Day. Her reasoning was, "It's what you do on the other 364 days of the year that matters most to me." That's fine, too. So, I respected her wishes and honored her that way.

Because Melissa's childhood was very difficult, I had to learn how to sacrificially serve her throughout our marriage. During her teenage years, her parent's divorce detrimentally affected her self-esteem. To compensate, she looked for love in all the wrong places and became more promiscuous than she wanted.

As if those heart-scars weren't enough, Melissa told me that when she was eight years old, her father molested her repeatedly for years. The irreparable damage it inflicted is impossible to fully reckon. She had dreadful flashbacks throughout our marriage and would often curl up into a little ball and just shake and shiver in the corner. I couldn't even go near her until she was ready. The lifelong scars of abuse are immeasurable.

All of this affected our intimate life significantly. It wasn't fair, and it wasn't our fault. Yet, we were stuck with it. We had to deal with it. I proceeded gently and tried carefully not to trample her delicate heart. I didn't always succeed and sometimes I blew it. Still, I determined to surrender my desires, give myself up, and tenderly care for Melissa through those harrowing flashback episodes. Understandably, it took years upon years for her to relinquish all the corners of her heart to me – to fully entrust it to a man again.

On our 10th Wedding Anniversary – just 20 months before she went to Heaven – Melissa gave me this note:

"My Dearest Robert,

I have lived a full life...more than most live their entire lives. ...I treasure your gifts of sacrifice in love, patience, understanding and forgiveness. You live daily what God commands you to – a true inspiration to any man who wants to be and see a good Godly husband. Thank you for loving me through difficult times. I know many times you have made the choice to love me – even though I made it very difficult. You are an example of sacrificial love to me. Thank you for your strength. ...I only hope I can return it – sacrificial love – to you completely as I learn from you. I love you. 10 years and counting... Happy Anniversary! -Your Melissa"

By serving Melissa sacrificially, we were still able to live a no-regrets marriage. After all she had been through, for her to say that she *"lived a full life"* is evidence of God's healing grace and proof of the power of serving your spouse sacrificially.

I'm still amazed how Inga loves a guy like me with a past such as mine. As a meticulous engineering type, I can be a real pain in the neck sometimes. Yet, she personifies patience and grace beyond measure with me. Inga sacrifices daily by respecting me and my past, and loving our family to no end.

Getting right with God and knowing Him personally enables us to get right with our spouse through sacrificial love and service. Peace in the home is the fruit that comes from a life of no regrets.

Below, I've listed some handy hints that can be put into practice every day. These ideas may not all be for you. Perhaps, just select a few to tackle the first month, then a few more the next. If you really want to improve, ask your spouse to gauge how well you are doing.

The men's list is much longer than the women's, possibly because (as someone once explained to me) man was the prototype, woman is the finished model. After all, God made man first – and then He fixed it!

Hopefully, these suggestions help keep your life of no regrets on track.

<u>Step 5 Action Points for *Women*</u>

1) Fall in love with Jesus so much that your husband notices.

2) Make a no-regrets decision to *Serve Your Husband Sacrificially*.

3) Tell him, "I love you!" every day.

4) Respect him with your words – in public and in private – even when he may not deserve it.

5) Encourage him to lead family prayers and Bible devotions.

6) Acknowledge and thank him for his sacrifices.

7) Kindly allow him to open doors for you.

8) Say phrases such as "You can do it!" and "I believe in you!" You help boost confidence and courage like none other. Let your words build up, not tear down. Nothing compares to your encouragement. Men need to know that we have what it takes. A wife is in a pivotal position to reinforce or destroy this. If reinforcement doesn't come from his wife, a man may make the horrible choice to seek it elsewhere.

9) Every once in a while, just do something to let him know he still melts your butter. It might just jump-start your intimacy all over again. Make him feel like your Superman, Zorro, or Indiana Jones who has come to rescue you. You'll never regret it.

Step 5 Action Points for *Men*

1) Fall in love with Jesus so much that your wife notices.

2) Make a no-regrets decision to *Serve Your Wife Sacrificially.*

3) Tell her, "I love you!" every day.

4) Don't ever let your wife out-serve you. You serve her. Focus on her needs, not your own – even if you receive nothing in return. Attend to her.

5) Cherish her as your queen with all you've got. She's worth it.

6) Cover her with words of adoration, affection, and affirmation.

7) Tell her, "You look beautiful!" every day. Let her know that you still think she's lovely, long after your wedding day.

8) Pray together and read Scripture with her daily.

9) Make friends with the phrase, "Yes, Dear."

10) If you have a point of contention, don't blurt everything before thinking. First, listen. Try to understand her before being understood.

11) When she has issues to discuss, listen quickly. Speak slowly. Proceed gently. Of course, you're probably exhausted, and the last thing you want is to hear another issue. Don't try to solve hers as you're so inclined. Just hold her and listen.

12) If she's had a rough day, give her a breather. If you have children, take them somewhere and give her a moment to herself.

13) Express your gratefulness to her daily for providing in so many ways. Don't take her for granted.

14) Speak nicely. Let your words build up, not tear down. Keep a kind tone in your voice over the phone. Zip your lip before you slip and say something you'll regret. Your unselfish attitude honors her and will avoid oodles of aggravation.

15) Write her surprise short love notes – enough to overflow a shoebox, e-mail, or text message box.

16) Rather than come home and plop down, get up instead, be involved and serve your wife. Marriage isn't for wimps.

17) Give her the remote and let her flip the TV channels. Go ahead. Give it up!

18) Phone your wife for no other reason except to say, "I Love You!" Don't add anything else such as, "...by the way, how about tacos for dinner?" Just focus on your love for her.

19) Court her regularly (weekly or monthly) and make all the arrangements for your date. Hold hands across the table as you eat and gaze into each other's eyes.

20) Do a special pleasantry for her that you've never done before. When was the last time you did something for the first time for her?

21) Don't let her enter a door without offering to open it first.

22) Help scoot her chair into place as she sits down.

23) Massage her feet at night before bedtime.

24) Warm up her side of the bed before she hops in.

25) Provide her with private time at the end of the day with a hot bubble-bath in a candle-lit room.

26) Surprise her with homemade breakfast in bed.

27) Kiss her for seven uninterrupted seconds every morning and evening.

28) Put toothpaste on her toothbrush every morning and evening.

29) Wipe off the bathroom counter after you drip your toothpaste or shaving cream all over it.

30) Replace the empty roll of toilet paper.

31) Close the toilet lid – every time.

32) Do the cooking, the dishes, the laundry, the cleaning. No whining! Serve sacrificially.

33) If she asks you to go shopping with her, smile and go along with a good attitude. No grumbling or sour complaining!

34) Make arrangements to periodically (perhaps once every one to four months) give her an afternoon, an evening, or a weekend away by herself or with her friends.

35) Bring home flowers and chocolates when she's not expecting it – even when you haven't spent the night in the dog house.

36) Romance her as she prefers to be treated.

37) Make her pleasure your primary passion during the intimacy of the marital embrace. During those romantic moments, it's not about you. It's all about her pleasure and satisfaction.

38) Never stop asking, "How can I best serve you?"

39) Remember: a happy wife – a happy life!

Step 6
Chapter Eleven

Today Counts

> *"Love the Lord your God with all your heart and with all your soul and with all your strength. These commandments that I give you today are to be upon your hearts. Impress them on your children. Talk about them when you sit at home and when you walk along the road, when you lie down and when you get up. Tie them as symbols on your hands and bind them on your foreheads. Write them on the door-frames of your houses and on your gates."*   (Deuteronomy 6:5-9 NIV)

"Daddy, can we build a birdhouse today?"

My 7-year-old daughter, Makenah, asked me this question early one Saturday morning as I was already knee-deep in a mile-long "honey-do" project list.

"Well…" I hesitated at first. With a home and four children under age eight, that perpetually pesky project list never dwindled. It secretly multiplied behind my back. I had tucked away those birdhouse instructions for weeks now, after promising Makenah we would build it "someday."

I paused a moment and took to heart our family mantra: "Let's make a memory!" With two special-needs children, I understood what it meant to cherish our children and savor even life's "mundane" moments.

"Someday" just arrived. I took a deep breath and relented.

"Okay, Makenah. Let's build that birdhouse!"

"Yeah!" she shouted, joined in a chorus of cheers by her younger brother, Nicholas.

We spent that afternoon building a birdhouse from spare cedar planks in the garage. Makenah colored it with arrows, directing the birds to the food. As we measured, cut, and pieced it together, our talk drifted to home-schooling.

After finishing first grade at the local school, Makenah actually asked *us* to home-school *her*. Melissa and I had carefully selected a curriculum and set up the classroom in the basement for autumn.

I was curious. "Makenah, why do you want to be home-schooled?"

Her response floored me.

"I just like you guys. I like being home with our family."

Whoa. In the midst of the flurry of life's "to-do" projects, time stood still.

We just experienced a miraculous moment that I'll treasure forever. Makenah genuinely loved us *that* much. If I hadn't intentionally set aside my agenda and invested quantity time with Makenah building that simple birdhouse, we never would have uncovered a priceless moment.

Just seven weeks later, Makenah's precious life was washed away in the flash flood, along with the rest of my family. However, that moment with her remains firmly embedded in my heart and memory. It resides there because I deliberately seized the opportunity to make a memory.

Amidst the perpetual pain of missing my heavenly family, I have peace because I cherished them while I could.

6th Step to No Regrets: *Cherish Your Family Intentionally.*

To live a life of no regrets with your family, it's vital to purposefully resolve in your heart to deliberately make a concerted effort to cherish them *intentionally*.

This axiom applies whether you have children or not. Cherish your family: your children, siblings, parents, grandparents, relatives, friends, church members, neighbors – whoever makes up your family. All of us can put this principle into practice.

Their life could end at any moment. It's essential to make every effort to redeem your time with them with purposeful intent.

After my family died, my grief gushed forth and cameras clamored to seize a slice of the story. My life of no regrets spilled over because we deliberately seized moments with our children.

Make a memory. You can always make more money. You can't always make more memories.

Time is a far more valuable currency than money. Eventually, you can get cash back. You can never get time back.

Children spell love: T.I.M.E.

You have to *take* the time with *undivided* attention (no electronic devices) to capture the moments.

You cannot plan or schedule these rare moments. You have to intentionally spend substantial time together. You have to be present to cherish their presence.

Your family wants you – now.

Perhaps you're gone a lot and try to compensate by purchasing material gifts as a substitute for your presence. Perhaps you really pile it on at birthdays or Christmas. Well, that's fine, but eventually they will forget your presents.

They'll remember your absence.

Nothing and no one can take the place of you. You are vital to them.

At my family's funeral, I was astounded at the number of people who showed up to pay their respects to support me. It was incredibly humbling, and I'm forever grateful. Yet, it amazes me how people always seem able to find time out of their hectic lives to attend a memorial service.

Please, hear these words of mine.

Don't wait until the next disaster, tragedy, or funeral to stop your schedule. Take time to spend with your family while you can.

Cherish your family. Cherish your children. Cherish them intentionally – now.

Make it count.

Today counts.

Live for today. Don't only plan for tomorrow. Live today as though there's no tomorrow. We are not guaranteed the next five seconds. Tomorrow may never come.

"Now listen to me, you that say, 'Today or tomorrow we will travel to a certain city, where we will stay a year and go into business and make a lot of money.' You don't even know what your life tomorrow will be! You are like a puff of smoke, which appears for a moment and then disappears. What you should say is this: 'If the Lord is willing, we will live and do this or that.'" (James 4:13-15 GNT)

The only time we truly have is right now. None of us is guaranteed tomorrow.

Children seem to catch this concept. They excel at it. I love how children plunge themselves into the moment of "now." It's almost as if they have no notion of tomorrow. Right now is all that matters – whether they're ecstatic, hungry, or reeling from a skinned knee.

Similar to sled riding when school is cancelled after winter's first big snow, children are immersed in "now." It's all about the snow and fun. Kids intentionally cherish the moment. They aren't worried about bills due next week, papers piled on the desk, or much less about school homework. They get it.

It's a great lesson for us to capture. As adults, we get so easily wrapped up in the cares and worries of tomorrow that we miss today. We miss "now." We miss our children. We blink and they're already grown and gone. We neglect to cherish our family intentionally.

I understand. Before I learned to intentionally cherish my family with no regrets, during seasons of more bills than income, I invested a lot of worry into those bills. I found that all my worry didn't pay off a single invoice. Furthermore, I missed a treasure chest of memorable moments in the process. My attitude of anguish plunged me into a wad of worry – rendering me incapable of savoring those moments with my family.

God doesn't want it to be that way. He longs to set us free from worry – just like those kids sledding – to cherish "now" in the most effective and fruitful way.

"So I tell you, don't worry about everyday life -- whether you have enough food, drink, and clothes. Doesn't life consist of more than food and clothing? Can all your worries add a single moment to your life? Of course not. So don't worry about having enough food or drink or clothing. ...Your heavenly Father already knows all your needs." (Matthew 6:25, 27, 31-32)

Children sense when parents are worried and agitated. It's contagious in the home, and it hampers our capacity to cherish our family. That's why knowing, worshipping, trusting, and obeying God is so vital. It brings peace to our lives and peace to our homes. God's peace is contagious. It provides the platform and the freedom to focus on savoring our family intentionally.

Peace emanates from a lifestyle of prayer, an attitude of gratitude, and surrendering to God as Lord of everyday life.

As a family, we pray out loud for skinned knees or even the ambulance whizzing by. At age two, Ezekiel could already pray "Amen!" anytime he fell and hurt himself. We thank God for our food and even pray over our pizza. We thank God for the beautiful day at the break of dawn and at nighttime. Before I drive off and before bedtime, I place my hand on their foreheads and pray a priestly blessing from the Old Testament. *"The Lord bless you and keep you; the Lord make his face shine upon you and be gracious to you; the Lord turn his face toward you and give you peace."* (Numbers 6:24-26 NIV)

Children discover God through their parents. To delight in them, cover them with prayers, and peacefully provide for them without worry directly reflects the way God cares for us. By living it daily, these faith lessons rarely need to be taught. They are usually caught.

The most important thing parents can do for their children is to love each other. Serve your spouse sacrificially. Live the Gospel in front of them. They'll get it.

My daughter, Makenah, left behind a handmade cardboard book she colored and assembled. Picture by picture, caption by caption, she detailed a time that groomed her faith.

One summer, we drove 100 miles into Kansas to visit Grandma on her farm. Makenah played with some delightful new beagle puppies. After sharing a bite to eat, we realized one of the puppies left the litter.

"Makenah, how about we pray that God helps us find the puppy. Okay?"

"Okay, Daddy. That's a great idea!"

Makenah and I prayed and then meandered down the gravel path. We called and whistled for the puppy as the mother beagle scurried left and right around our feet. We crossed the road into the corn field and called again.

"Here, Puppy!" Makenah yelled, at the top of her seven-year-old voice.

"Wait a minute, Makenah. I hear something."

We both stopped in our tracks and listened. Beyond several rows of corn, we heard a rustling in the stalks, and then a yelping. The mother beagle leapt ahead of us as we scampered to catch up. Within moments, we found the two of them reunited between rows of corn stalks, joyfully licking each other's fur.

Makenah's handmade book unfolded this story, frame by frame. She ended it with, "God found it. He saved the puppy! Prayer works."

She got it. Makenah caught it. By living our faith in plain everyday life, and by intentionally taking the time with my daughter to search for her baby beagle friend, she learned a profound life lesson about God and prayer.

If I had ignored Makenah or sloughed off the sad look in her eyes when she first realized the missing puppy, we would have missed this moment. I would have missed this memory. My daughter would have missed this timely faith lesson.

Make it a point to cherish your family intentionally. Build the birdhouse today. Pass along your faith. Seize every possible moment. As you do, it will inevitably give birth to miraculous moments – to help capture and convey those timeless faith lessons.

It takes more than elaborate vacations. As parents, it takes deliberate choices in everyday life: eating meals together, walking around the block, going to the store, searching for the puppy, or even fixing the car together. I've found that these everyday settings and blocks of time naturally give birth to remarkable moments.

In the dusty details of everyday family life, filled with seemingly mundane moments and dirty diapers, we can still intentionally choose to purposely share deliberate time together – to capture and cherish those irreplaceable memories.

It may only be a moment, a flicker, or barely a second: when you are walking down the lane and see a shooting star together; when you are fishing and your child finally opens up and shares his heart; when you are doing dishes or changing the oil together; or when you are eating at the kitchen table and everyone bursts into spontaneous laughter. Those moments only emerge by investing intentional time.

A kitchen table is a wonderful starting place. Ours had seen so much life: spills, bills, stains, nicks and knots, birthdays and holidays, turkeys, cookies, cakes, pizza, parties, and ice cream. A kitchen table is such a simple object and yet such a powerful force in a home. If it is rejected, it can scatter and scramble a family as they eat apart at different times and places on the run. The television can drain the very conversation and life from a household. When you eat together, turn off the TV and turn on your family.

If the kitchen table is embraced and accepted, its magnetic capacity can draw a family into a cohesive unit as none other. Coupled with the sounds, sights, textures, and aromatic culinary wonders, the mealtime experience can create moments and memories that endure a lifetime.

As best you can amidst errands and activities, try to sit down as a family and have at least one meal together each day. You'll never regret it.

Growing up, mealtimes around our table comprised some of my fondest memories. With all ten of us there sitting elbow to elbow on benches, my father often remarked that the only way he knew we had company was if he heard, "Could you please pass the ketchup, Mr. Rogers?"

My parents made a point to keep the TV off and even unplug the phone lines. This was long before cell phones. They figured, "If we were out eating in a restaurant, nobody could call us anyway." That stuck with me because it demonstrated how important it was to share a meal without distractions or interruptions.

Do your family a favor. Turn your personal electronic devices down at mealtime. Unplug. Cherish those moments and let your family know they are worth your time and undivided attention.

"If you fail to plan, you plan to fail," so the saying goes. Plan solid blocks of continuous, uninterrupted time with them. Let them know how much they deserve your undivided devotion and turn off your phone, tablet, and

TV. You can't hear the cries of your children's hearts with one ear plastered to the speaker. You'll miss the longing expressions in their eyes with one eye fixated on the display screen.

Involve your children in chores around the house and yard. Don't just slough them off. It may take you longer to finish, but they are worth your extra time. Nicholas always said, "Hey, Dad, can I help you?" Already, Ezekiel loves brooms, shovels, and screwdrivers. He incessantly asks if we can mop, sweep, shovel, or vacuum together. He's made friends with Windex as we clean the windows or wash the car together. It melts my heart while we're mopping together and he says out of the blue, "I love you, Daddy."

Many children have no idea what their parents do outside the home. Bring them to your office and introduce them to your associates.

Take your children to work with you or on errands. You will cherish that priceless time together. I regularly take mine to the hardware store for a mini "date." We stop for a sundae or special treat afterwards. It gives my wife some well-deserved alone time for herself, too.

Growing up, my mom accompanied her dad selling horseradish to the delis around town. Likewise, my siblings and I spent many Saturdays with Grandpa at the city market in Cincinnati selling fresh horseradish. More than once, Melissa showed up with a pizza and a blanket at my workplace. Our children plopped down, and we had a pizza picnic lunch. I take my children on road-trips regularly. Ezekiel and Estellah accompany me as we share our family's story.   Since age two, Ezekiel still loves handing bookmarks to people as they depart.

Keep their hearts close.   Involve your children frequently and don't live unilateral lives.   Build a deeply embedded   rapport   with   them   to   help   foster communication – especially during critical teen years. Quantity time together can reinforce and affirm children, keeping those crucial lines of communication flowing.

Children need to know their hearts are safe – that they can share about anything with active, unconditional love and listening.   The more time you spend with them, the safer they feel sharing anything with you without fear of retribution or judgment in return.   That won't happen without intentionally investing in sizeable family time.

If   parents   don't   spend   substantial   time communicating with their children, someone else will. They'll learn values – right off the internet.

Deliberately spend generous time with your family – listening, sharing stories, and teaching Scriptures – and behold the quality moments which unfold.   Quality comes from quantity.

"Make good use of every opportunity you have..." (Ephesians 5:16 GNT)

Live to love your family – not your job, paycheck, habits, or hobbies.   Don't be consumed by promotions, careers, or activities.   It's so easy to let two more hours slip by at the office or in the garage tinkering with toys. That work will still be there tomorrow.   Your children may not.   If you're not careful, they may slip by your life.

Don't blink.   Life is fast.   Life is fragile.

Chapter Twelve

"Someday" is Today

"Treasure the importance of families. Savor every, single precious minute with your spouses and children. Hug and kiss them every day, every morning and every evening. Tell them over and over how much you love them. Snuggle with them at bedtime. Place your hand on their heads and bless them every day as I did." (Robert Rogers at his first press conference: September 1, 2003, in Emporia, Kansas.)

Just two days after the flash flood, while I was still in Kansas, the police asked me to give a press conference. I had just identified Makenah, and they were still searching for Melissa. I urged families to cherish one another intentionally.

I've played piano for many weddings and witnessed countless fathers-of-the-bride break down in tears as they escort her down the aisle and give her away – overcome with regrets – mortified at the sudden realization that it's too late. He missed her life. She grew up without him. He spent his life at the office. Rather than working to live, he lived to work.

"Someday" never came because he was never there to grasp it.

Too many parents spend the majority of their lives away from home – not cherishing their family – only to realize that their children have grown and left home without them.

When I worked as a design engineer at Honeywell Aviation, I thought it might be fun to enroll in their "Learn to Fly" program for employees. I attended six weeks of ground school and received my certificate. However, when I considered the hefty requirements for flying lessons and the hourly price tag, I realized it essentially amounted to an expensive hobby – alone. Compared to my family, it meant nothing. I could spend that time and money much more fruitfully with my wife and children. I opted out of the flight lessons and intentionally chose to cherish my family. I have no regrets.

Don't trade diamonds for stones. Don't miss it.

Prioritize God 1st, family 2nd, and everything else a distant 3rd. It's not about you. It's all about your relationships – beginning with God and your family.

When I walk through neighborhoods, I notice many beautifully manicured lawns. Every shrub and blade of grass is groomed meticulously. Sometimes people tend to their turf daily. That's fine. I pray they cherish their family at least more than their yard. After all, at the end of the day, it's just grass. It's sown, it's grown, it's mown, it's blown, and it's gone.

"As for man, his days are like grass, he flourishes like a flower of the field; the wind blows over it and it is gone, and its place remembers it no more." (Psalm 103:15-16 NIV)

My father spent 25 years in broadcasting in Cincinnati. During his time at the ABC TV affiliate, he advanced through the ranks quickly and was promoted to National Sales Manager and soon offered a VP position. Realizing it would involve moving our family to Chicago and spending excessive time away from us, he made a monumental no-regrets decision and declined the offer. Instead, he took a substantial pay cut to accept a position at the fledgling PBS station in town.

Mom and Dad never had much money, but every Christmas, they still somehow managed to come up with a live tree and presents underneath it. I'll take that any day over a bigger house near a bigger city with an absent father. No regrets, indeed.

My father also made a no-regrets decision after his father died of cancer and smoking related complications, exacerbated by alcohol. One day, our family doctor confronted Dad, then a three-pack-a-day smoker. In the doctor's office he bluntly asked, "Do you want to live to see your children grow up?" Dad's mouth opened, and his jaw slammed the floor. He realized immediately what he had to do in order to cherish his eight children intentionally. He quit smoking cold-turkey. He did it out of sheer will and determination, resolved to live a life of no regrets.

My father also cherished his children intentionally in a different way. He came out of a verbally abusive home on the part of his father. So, Dad made it a point never to raise his voice in our home. He intentionally cherished each of us wholesomely. What an incredible gift to children to break a cycle of abuse!

Likewise, Melissa also made a no-regrets decision to cherish our family in a wholesome way. Growing up, even though she was repeatedly abused physically, and later witnessed the anguish and anger which accompanied her parents' bankruptcy and subsequent divorce, she resolved with great determination to end the cycle of abuse. She and I intentionally cherished our children every way conceivable.

I've heard it said that over-commitment is a primary destroyer of families and marriages. We all tend to think we can do more than time allows. Everything in life takes more time and costs more money than we expect. We sign up for this and get involved in that. Before we know it, we've diluted our marriage and family time so much that all they get are our scraps.

I made this mistake early on in marriage. I was heavily involved at church playing piano for various services, choirs, and classes. It required many rehearsal nights and most of Sunday. On top of my demanding high-tech job in Silicon Valley, I was robbing my family of time and devotion. I asked our worship leader what to do. He shared priceless words of wisdom I'll never forget.

"Robert, family is your first ministry."

He was absolutely right. On their own, none of the activities in which I was involved were inherently bad. As a whole, they were detrimental to our family. I had to let go of several commitments.

I was doing a lot of right things, but I wasn't doing things right.

Over-commitment can often be a pitfall of any job or benevolent work – even church or ministry. It's natural to feel that doing good things must mean it is all good. However, if we lose our family in the process, what have we accomplished? More harm than good.

Often, we garner significance at work from accomplishments. How much did I get done today? How big was the promotion, the account, or the bonus? How many things did I check off my list? I understand that motivation, but don't ever sacrifice your children, spouse, or family to advance your career. Resist building your own empire of accomplishments and wealth. Instead, focus on building your family and God's Kingdom. When you do, God will take care of the rest. (Matthew 6:33)

"Instead, store up riches for yourselves in heaven… For your heart will always be where your riches are." (Matthew 6:20-21 GNT)

Often, it's so easy to become strictly goal-focused that we forget to be family-focused. *"You cannot serve both God and money. …God knows your hearts. For the things that are considered of great value by people are worth nothing in God's sight."* (Luke 16:13, 15 GNT)

Don't be so busy making a living that you neglect to make a life.

Children especially have a keen ability to discern whether we love our careers more than them. Is it money or family? Children know. We cannot serve both.

Please, let my story be your reminder, if necessary. Do you truly want to live a life of no regrets? Keep your priorities. Hold your family's hearts close to yours.

Don't live to work. Work to live. *"Be wise enough not to wear yourself out trying to get rich."* (Proverbs 23:4 GNT)

Don't work so hard to keep your stuff, job, and money that you lose your family. God doesn't mind if you have things, but He does mind if those things have you. Possessions should be rightfully gained, but very loosely held. It's a precept of Christianity: what you keep, you lose; what you lose, you keep. (Matthew 10:39, Luke 17:33, John 12:25)

Too often, parents blow it. They seek better jobs, bigger houses, and more stuff at the expense of their family. *"Such is the fate of all who are greedy for gain. It ends up robbing them of life."* (Proverbs 1:19) It takes deliberate, concerted effort to cherish your family intentionally, spend substantial time together, and glean those no-regrets moments.

I intentionally chose not to work sixty or eighty-hour weeks. I easily could have. There was always more work than I could finish in a day. I discovered something, though; it was still on my desk the next morning. It didn't go anywhere. If enough work exists for eighty hours each week, then they need to hire another employee. I refuse to compromise my family to work double time when I'm only paid for one. Our time and their lives are not for sale. They are priceless. Besides, God is big enough to provide our needs from a reasonable work week.

Come home from work on time. Don't have an affair with your career. Don't spend your best time and energy at the office. *"Give to Caesar what is Caesar's."* (Matthew 22:21 NIV) Give to the office what belongs at the office. Please, don't just give your family your leftover remnants at the end of a long day. They deserve much better. Careers and hobbies come after family.

Next to God, I'm addicted to my family. From the moment I drive off, I live for coming home. I eagerly anticipate pulling into the driveway, tackling them at the door, and greeting them with a great big "Hiiiiiiii!"

Give your best to those you love most. When you arrive home, greet them with an enthusiastic smile, hug, and "I love you!" If you've had a difficult day, be kind and gentle with your spouse and children. If you lose your temper, ask forgiveness and extend grace right away. *Every* day, no matter how thorny, is a precious, fragile gift. None of us is guaranteed tomorrow.

I realize there are days we can all get on each other's last nerves. Sometimes it's all you can do to get everyone into bed in one piece. At the end of the day, let all the rough stuff roll off your back, take a deep breath, and thank God for another day.

Make "rocking chair" decisions, so that one day, when you are older and rocking in your chair, you'll look back and confidently say, "I'm grateful I made that decision. I'm glad I didn't spend more time at the office. I'm thankful I spent more time with my family."

In order to say "Yes" to God and your family, you may have to say "No" to something else: no to yourself, no to working late, no to your hobby, no to another project, no to temptation. Ask God to reveal areas that need adjustments and obey His prompting immediately.

Be alert, aware, and available to seize family times. Too many parents passively let the days drift by and pass up teachable moments, miraculous memories, and priceless opportunities. It's vital to actively engage our families, particularly in our faith. Parents have the awesome responsibility of ensuring that our families reach eternity.

I wonder if one of God's questions to us as parents when we get to Heaven will be, "Where are the rest of them?" Our most essential mission is to get our family to Heaven. If we miss that, we miss it all.

Husbands, be the priest of your home. Lead your family in prayer and cover them with daily Scripture reading. If you don't, then you're leaving the front door wide open for the Thief to come in to steal and destroy. (John 10:10) See to it that they know God personally.

Men, meet your wife's and children's needs before your own. Intentionally nurture and cherish them. Actively listen, speak, and look eye-to-eye with them. Be an integral part of their day, not just someone who passively comes and goes to work each day. Love their mother with all you've got.

Love Jesus with all of your heart. If Christ truly has all of your heart, then your wife will be the most honored, cherished, and spoiled woman on the face of the planet – because you lay down your life for your wife. Furthermore, your children will see a daddy who becomes more like Jesus every day.

The overall tone we strive to maintain in our family is one of fun, love, respect, and personal relationship with Jesus Christ. We do our best to transform what some might consider mundane activities into sacred memories.

Rather than a meal, have a picnic. Rather than a movie, have family fun nights with popcorn, pizza, movies, and ice cream! Rather than an errand, it's a date. Rather than a chore, it's a chance to work and talk together. Rather than "go to bed," play music, sing, dance, read, discuss the day, or recite Scripture. Rather than just a job, it's a means to realize your heart's desire: the treasure of a happy and healthy family.

Find a simple way to celebrate your family every day. When they wake up, set the tone for the day and declare joyfully, *"This is the day the Lord has made; let us rejoice and be glad in it."* (Psalm 118:24 NIV) Worship as a family. Keep them in the pew with you at church, if at all possible. Hang their artwork around the house and celebrate their creativity. Go on a walk, shoot hoops, or ride bikes together. Attend their school functions, graduations, dances, and skating parties. Show up at their music and dance recitals. Cheer at their sports games. Be their biggest fan. Exude a zest and thrill about your children, your family, and Almighty God. Not only will your kids notice, but others will, too.

Tell your children that you believe in them; they can do it; they can do all things through Christ who gives them strength. (Philippians 4:13) Say, "You are my beloved child. In you I am well pleased." (Matthew 3:17) "You are precious, you are honored, and I love you." (Isaiah 43:4) Let your sons know how mighty they are and your daughters know how lovely they look.

Capture picture, video, and audio family moments. With today's gadgets, it's easier than ever.

Above all, try not to get your feathers ruffled too easily. I've found it's just not worth getting upset when life happens.

Cherish your family instead. Make friends with the phrase, "No problem. It's no big deal." If your two-year-old dumps a gallon of cooking oil on the kitchen linoleum and tops it off with the box of Cheerios, just laugh and say, "No problem, Zachary. It's no big deal." You just made a memory. If you ask your four-year-old to run downstairs and grab a roll of toilet paper, and he returns with the end of a long strand strung up the stairs and all the way through the house, laugh out loud and say, "Thank you, Ezekiel!" You made another unforgettable memory.

Even though Melissa had a degree in Interior Design, she deeply desired to stay at home with our children. So, we lived a simple and frugal lifestyle as I supported a family of six on a modest income of one. It was one of the best no-regrets decisions we ever made. Melissa was first to admit it. She frequently referred to our decision to forego her extra income, stay at home to raise our four children, and tighten our belts to live off one salary as the "best decision we ever made," indeed.

Intentionally use your creativity to live life to the full. An abundance of simple, spontaneous, and affordable activities are at your fingertips to make priceless memories. Open your eyes to the amenities around you. To help stir your thoughts, here are just a few to consider.

Go on individual dates with your children simply over a cheap bowl of chili or ice cream. Find low-cost tickets to the ballpark, symphony, or ballet and take your children on dates there, too. Park near the airport and watch the planes take off and land. Hop aboard a train depot several stops away and ride the rails into town. Roam around the train station, eat a sack lunch, and ride the train back a few hours later. What great memories for a paltry price!

On hot summer nights, we set up a small inflatable pool out back and enjoy pizza and popsicles as our kids cheer, "To infinity and beyond!" before diving in, belly first. We go backyard camping or at local parks within an hour of home – sometimes with just one child, to give them our undivided attention. Even though I'm a lousy fisherman, I still take my children and do my best. We don't catch much, but we make memories and have a blast trying.

I once took Zachary and Nicholas fishing at a nearby park where we caught our first and only fish – ever. The lake had a four-mile bike path around it. After our picnic lunch, I towed my boys behind me in a bike trailer, and we made fabulous afternoon memories. I even utilized a nearby county lake with free oar-boats for fishing, as well as another lake with inexpensive aluminum rental boats with outboard motors. Neither was fast or fancy, but the memories with my sons were priceless and irreplaceable.

I'm nowhere near perfect. I don't nail all this on the head every day. I'm still working at it. I live a life of no regrets because this is my guiding goal. If you aim for nothing, you'll hit it every time.

On December 20, 2009, as I gave Ezekiel and Estellah a bath, I finished the final suds from a Johnson's Baby Shampoo bottle that I had opened over six years earlier in Missouri to bathe my heavenly family. It was packed away when I moved in 2006, and Inga and I later uncovered it. The words on the side of the bottle said it all. They struck my heart in a poignant way as I noticed the ironic slogan, "No more tears." Yes, indeed. I cherished Makenah, Zachary, Nicholas, and Alenah intentionally then as I do Ezekiel and Estellah now.

Two days later, Ezekiel and I went sledding at dusk to bask ourselves in the "now." After we crashed at the bottom and flipped onto our backs, I looked up into the night sky and whispered, "Thank you, Lord, for moments like these."

After the dreadful miscarriage and burial of our little Dale in September 2009, Inga and I joyfully discovered around Christmastime that we were expecting another child again! Since each birth and miscarriage so far involved serious complications, we scheduled a C-Section delivery this time. On August 16th of 2010, God blessed us with another strapping son whom we named "Leo George" – after Inga's grandpa Leo and my father, George. At 7-pounds, 3-ounces, and 20-inches long, his name means, "A man of the earth with the strength of a lion who gathers an abundant harvest."

Tears of thanksgiving poured from our eyes as we clutched Leo tightly in our arms – nearly a year after losing our little Dale so traumatically. God is still good and still gives life. He restored in His way and in His time, and He *"saw that it was good."* (Genesis 1:4)

Then, on March 12th of 2012, God graced us once again with a lovely, healthy, 8-pound, 21-inch daughter we named, "Lola Elizabeth" meaning, "Compassionate one - consecrated to God."

My knees hit the floor at Lola's birth – as they do most every morning – in thanksgiving for our four children to behold on this planet. Not once did we inquire or discover their gender before birth, and yet God remarkably saw fit to bless Inga and me in this incomprehensible way.

In 2003, my precious wife, two mighty sons, and two lovely daughters perished in the Kansas flash flood. Ten years later in 2013, somehow, God has graced me with a precious wife, two mighty sons and two lovely daughters. How can this be? *"Humanly speaking, it is impossible. But with God everything is possible."* (Matthew 19:26)

"Taste and see that the LORD is good. Oh, the joys of those who trust in him!" (Psalm 34:8)

I love and cherish my family beyond words – intentionally.

"When I think of the wisdom and scope of God's plan, I fall to my knees and pray to the Father, the Creator of everything in heaven and on earth. Now glory be to God! By his mighty power at work within us, he is able to accomplish infinitely more than we would ever dare to ask or hope." (Ephesians 3:14-15, 20)

God is faithful. He is a God of Restoration. He did it for Job. He's done it for me. He can do it for you.

"Teach us to make the most of our time..." (Psalm 90:12) Redeem the time you have with your families. That time is now. Live your dreams with them immediately, not tomorrow, next year, or "someday" when you get around to it.

"Someday" is today.

Today counts.

Engraved on every tombstone is a dash between the birth date and the death date. That little dash represents a life. We only get one dash between the dates. There are no dash do-overs. Everyone dies. Make your dash count.

Immerse yourself in the moments. Savor them, whether cheerful or challenging. They are still moments to experience together. Make a memory. Live a life of no regrets with your family. Cherish them intentionally, every day.

Step 6 Action Points

1) Make a no-regrets decision to *Cherish Your Family Intentionally.*

2) Make a daily discipline to celebrate your family some way, every day.

3) Pray together and read Scripture with your family.

4) Take the time; capture the moments with undivided attention (no electronic gadgets).

5) Skip the worry; savor the memories.

6) Don't trade diamonds for stones.

7) Come home on time. Don't live to work; work to live.

8) Don't be so busy making a living that you neglect to make a life.

9) Sit down and have an "unplugged" dinner together (no TV or personal electronic devices).

10) Take your children on errands or to work with you.

11) Be creative. Turn mundane moments into sacred memories.

12) Turn off the TV and turn on your family.

13) Keep your children's hearts close.

14) Family is your 1st ministry.

15) Don't give your family your leftovers.

16) Make "rocking chair" decisions.

17) Make a memory.

18) Make today count.

Step 7
Chapter Thirteen

Set Free

"Lord...how many times do I have to forgive...
Seven times?' 'No, not seven times,' answered Jesus, 'but
seventy times seven.'"   (Matthew 18:21-22 GNT)

"Get over it!"

These three words reverberated in my mind as a dear friend once challenged me.

"Get over it. Let it go."

I thought, "Are you kidding me? Do you know what they did to me?"

Then my thoughts immediately turned to Melissa and her father. Her situation made my predicament seem miniscule. Even after years of molestation, Melissa let it go.

She forgave him.

Through reconciliation and many years of counseling, she somehow got past that horrific offense of abuse. Her example inspired me to forgive him. Every time the flashbacks snuck into our marriage and affected our intimate lives, we both forgave him again.

Melissa still loved her father and showed it every time he came to visit. She made his favorite tapioca pudding and stirred in melted chocolate chips. Their relationship steadily healed and flourished beautifully. It allowed him to become a marvelous grandpa to our four children. He was even there at the Kansas City airport when we arrived home from China down the jet-way with Alenah in our arms.

Because Melissa forgave him repeatedly, the sins of the past no longer had a hold on her. She died with a clean heart and no regrets.

7th Step to No Regrets: *Forgive Others Repeatedly.*

I've heard many times that forgiveness is when I give up my right to hurt you for hurting me. That's exactly what Melissa did for her father. She forgave and gave up her right. No matter how many times it took, she kept forgiving – repeatedly. It gave her freedom to live and love again. Gradually, she was able to fully trust again. She was able to love me and grew to love her father more deeply than ever before.

She demonstrated that what happens *through* you is far more important than what happens *to* you. Forgiveness permeated through her, from deep within her soul, deeper than the scars of abuse. As her forgiving words and deeds arose through her being, they brushed against the scars and brought healing to the wounds.

Through forgiveness, Melissa's tribulation brought forth transformation.

I witnessed it firsthand. In 1990, before I first drove out to her father's hog farm in Kansas to ask permission to marry his daughter, Melissa and her father were still estranged and hadn't spoken in years. Thirteen years later when Melissa went to Heaven in 2003, they were completely restored. That's the power of repeated forgiveness. That's no regrets.

Life will inevitably wound you. It's vital not to stay stuck in your scars. Don't remain paralyzed in your pain. Let God in – to restore your soul – to heal you. If you're still clutching offenses, betrayals, guilt, or unforgiveness, the only person you're hurting is you.

When you don't forgive, you don't have freedom. That person who offended you still has an effect over you. You're empowering them. When you choose to forgive, it relinquishes that person's influence and control over your life. It gives your freedom back. It restores your liberty to live.

The longer you hold onto the offense, the longer that person holds onto you. They maintain influence and authority over your life. Don't hold onto offenses, grudges, or bitterness. Don't allow bitterness to even take root. *"Get rid of all bitterness, passion, and anger. No more shouting or insults, no more hateful feelings of any sort. Instead, be kind and tender-hearted to one another, and forgive one another, as God has forgiven you through Christ."* (Ephesians 4:31-32 GNT)

In fact, don't even let a day go by with unforgiveness or bitterness in your heart – especially towards your spouse or family. Don't lay down your head on the pillow if you are mad at one other. Work it out. Get over it! Whatever it takes, don't let the sun go down on your differences. *"Go and be reconciled to that person.*

Come to terms quickly with your enemy before it is too late..." (Matthew 5:24-25)

Jesus put the utmost premium on forgiving: *"...they crucified Jesus there... Jesus said, 'Forgive them, Father! They don't know what they are doing.'"* (Luke 23:33-34 GNT) Jesus held nothing back. He sacrificed everything for us – His broken body and shed blood on the cross. Even after He felt His own Father had abandoned Him (Matthew 27:46), He somehow still mustered the mercy within Himself to forgive those who crucified Him. If Jesus freely forgave at that moment, then so should we – anytime.

Jesus also promised, *"If you forgive those who sin against you, your heavenly Father will forgive you. But if you refuse to forgive others, your Father will not forgive your sins."* (Matthew 6:14-15) Imagine God not forgiving you. That is big-time regrets! Our unforgiveness binds God's hands.

Grudges smother our prayers. They eat away at the human soul as a cancer. Jesus said that we *"can pray for anything... But when you are praying, first forgive anyone you are holding a grudge against..."* (Mark 11:24-25) Unforgiveness douses our prayers with the poison of bitterness, rendering them useless. *"If I had not confessed the sin in my heart, my Lord would not have listened."* (Psalm 66:18) Unforgiveness creeps into our words and seeps through our eyes. It manifests through every crevice of our lives. It's palpable in a person's countenance and conversation.

Forgiveness, on the other hand, radiates peace through a person's face and tranquility in their words. As the saying goes, forgiveness sets a captive free: me.

In the Old Testament, Job's friends initially came to comfort him, but ended up accusing him of his own

family's deaths. As if Job's pain wasn't bad enough –
losing his family, his business, and his health – he
demonstrated forgiveness above it all. *"When Job prayed for
his friends, the Lord restored his fortunes. In fact, the Lord gave
him twice as much as before!"* (Job 42:10)

Job's act of forgiveness granted grace and mercy,
and released him from the prison of bitterness.
Furthermore, it released God's double blessings on his
life. Job's mercy activated God's grace.

I've attended numerous enriching Bible study
courses at The Cove: the Billy Graham Training Center in
beautiful Asheville, North Carolina. During one class
after an evening session, the instructor explained how
sometimes people wound us deeply, like a knife in the
stomach. Other times, we don't see it coming and the
knife in our back feels like betrayal. He challenged us all
to forgive those who wounded or betrayed us, even if that
meant forgiving God.

Our instructor encouraged us to figuratively grab
hold of those knives and pull them out. Tears of
repentance flowed across the room as many cried audibly.
I fell to my knees, weeping. I was convicted of not
forgiving God. I felt as though He had betrayed me by
allowing my family to die.

Our instructor then said something astounding.
"Someone here tonight has more knives to pull out.
There are five knives in your back."

We had never spoken before, and he knew
nothing of my story. Yet, he was spot on. He was talking
about me: five knives represented my five family
members. I had to pull all five knives out and forgive
God for each one.

God is God and cannot sin. He did no wrong. Still, I had to forgive repeatedly and let Him off the hook, as it were, for all the deaths in my life. As I did, I felt an enormous weight lift.

It healed me. It liberated me. I was free.

Perhaps you feel wounded or betrayed. Perhaps the perpetrator was a trusted friend, a relative, the Church, or even God. I encourage you to take a moment right now and kneel before God. Breathe in deeply, literally grab the handle of that symbolic knife, and pull it out as you exhale. Let all the venom and bitterness ooze out. As best you can, say these words:

"I forgive you."

"Please forgive me."

"I surrender all."

Now, let it go.

Breathe out the bitterness. Breathe in Jesus.

Breathe out you. Breathe in mercy.

Let Him in to heal your wounds.

Begin anew.

He can and He will if you allow Him. If you forgive others repeatedly, healing and restoration will flow through your life. I've experienced it and know it to be true.

King David experienced it. *"When I refused to confess my sin, I was weak and miserable, and I groaned all day long. Finally, I confessed all my sins to you and stopped trying to hide them. ...And you forgave me! All my guilt is gone."* (Psalm 32:3, 5)

Unforgiveness binds you in the chains of regrets. It padlocks you in the prison of your past.

Perhaps you feel guilty over something you should've, could've, or would've done. Perhaps you are guilty of infidelity towards your spouse. Perhaps you've sinned against God or someone else. By all means, ask forgiveness for your transgressions from those you wounded. Ask God to forgive you. Seek repentance through confession – the Sacrament of Reconciliation.

Perhaps someone offended or betrayed you. Maybe you even feel God or the Church has wounded you. Forgive them, too, repeatedly.

To forgive others repeatedly also includes forgiving yourself.

Take a moment right now and forgive yourself.

We serve a God of second chances. If you've done wrong, He is willing to forgive you and give you a new start. For, *"if we confess our sins to God, he will keep his promise and do what is right: he will forgive us our sins and purify us from all our wrongdoing."* (1 John 1:9 GNT)

Don't wallow in a puddle of pity forever. Don't be gripped by guilt. Let the past be past. When we are forgiven, God casts our sins into the ocean and remembers them no more. *"You will be merciful to us once again. You will trample our sins underfoot and send them to the bottom of the sea!"* (Micah 7:19 GNT)

If God lets it go, then so should I. *"As far as the east is from the west, so far does he remove our sins from us."* (Psalm 103:12 GNT) Retain only enough to prevent you from committing it again. Forget everything else.

If you have regrets over a past decision, cut yourself some slack. Let yourself off the hook. Don't continually and repeatedly beat yourself up over questions of should've, could've, or would've. No matter how hard you try, you'll never get to the bottom of those lingering questions.

Your past is past. You can't change it. Let today be your first day living a life of no regrets.

As a meticulous engineer, I dissected and scrutinized umpteen times every aspect and element of the night my family died – from every possible angle. I tried to uncover what caused us to be at the very epicenter of impact of that wall of water, or how we could have avoided it. Perhaps if we hadn't gone for ice cream, or filled up on gas, or what if…?

The litany and line of questions are endless. You'll never solve them within the confines of your own mind. They likely will never be answered this side of Heaven.

So, let them go.

Surrender your questions to God. When we surrender our lives to God, He doesn't owe us any explanations.

Just let His peace enter in.

In my feeble attempts to ask the questions and unravel the answers, here's what I discovered.

God is bigger.

God is bigger than it all.

He knew all of the various variables that affected our thoughts and timing that night of August 30, 2003. He could have easily thwarted or adjusted any one of them to prevent the final outcome. Yet, He didn't. It happened. God didn't stop it. He *"...allowed me to suffer much hardship..."* (Psalm 71:20) I had to let God off the hook and believe that somehow He *"...will restore me to life again and lift me up from the depths of the earth."* (Psalm 71:20)

God allowed His own son, Jesus, to die – for the greatest good. He allowed Lazarus to die, too – for a greater purpose. Just as He loved Lazarus, God deeply loved our family. We followed Him daily. Still, God allowed them to die.

He foresaw it all and has something good in store – a purpose beyond what our finite minds can fathom. Perhaps *"God is protecting them from the evil to come."* (Isaiah 57:1) Whatever the reason, God knew and already planned for a great ultimate outcome.

Perhaps your child died or committed suicide. Perhaps they left you or their faith. Perhaps you feel partially responsible or that you could have prevented it.

What I found is that those who are able to forgive themselves and forgive God radiate peace and even joy from their countenance. *"Those who look to him for help will be radiant with joy; no shadow of shame will darken their faces."* (Psalm 34:5) They epitomize no regrets. Those who are still stuck in the groove of questioning and condemnation exude only bitterness and resentfulness.

Let it go.

Give it up to God.

Place it in His hands and settle in the simple realization that He is God, and you are not. That's that. Get out of your rut.

When you don't forgive yourself, it's similar to an old record player whose needle is endlessly stuck in the groove on a vinyl LP. You beat yourself up when you repeatedly condemn yourself over and over. It's likely taking a toll and annoying you, your family, and those around you. It's reducing your effectiveness for God. It's possibly even causing you to miss out on God's perfect plan for you – because you're still wrapped up in the past and you haven't moved on to the present or future.

It's time to pop that scratchy record off the player and listen to something else.

If Christ doesn't condemn, then neither should you.

Start listening to God by reading His Word. Stop condemning yourself. Catch the revelation that *"There is no condemnation now for those who live in union with Christ Jesus."* (Romans 8:1 GNT)

Chapter Fourteen

Redemption

"Forgive us the wrongs we have done, as we forgive the wrongs that others have done to us."
(Matthew 6:12 GNT)

In the fall of 2007, I received a sobering call that Melissa's father was diagnosed with stage-four bone cancer. The doctors estimated one month to live. With the tenacity of a bulldog, he fought to survive with his gracious wife at his side and every available treatment.

In the spring of 2008, against all odds, he showed remarkable improvement. Inga, Ezekiel, and I were in Kansas City one weekend. I was exhausted from ministering five times in two days. Still, I had a sense to call and check in, since he was only 100 miles away.

Ezekiel – only eight months old – desperately needed a nap, all of us were weary, and we had every reason to bag the whole idea. We wanted to just head to bed and crash. In our spirit of "no regrets," we decided to go ahead and visit.

So, on Sunday afternoon, April 6, 2008, Inga, Ezekiel, and I drove through Kansas farmland to visit Melissa's father. Inga saw the farm where they grew up, the high school, and the Sonic where Melissa waitressed. Inga handled it all with unwavering grace.

We pulled into the nursing home, took a deep breath, and prayed.

"Lord, please help us say the right things. Please let this be a healing visit."

I asked the front desk for his room number. Inga and I approached slowly, and I tapped on the door.

"Hello? Are you in there, wild man?"

"Robert? Is that you, wild man?"

To my pleasant surprise, though his voice was weak and his limbs were terribly thin, he looked remarkably well and was full of smiles and stories.

"I'd like to introduce you to my wife, Inga, and our son, Ezekiel."

It was a powerfully seminal moment for us all. For Melissa's father to meet the woman who married his son-in-law after his daughter's death; to meet Ezekiel and witness a living picture of God's restoration power was remarkably profound.

Melissa's brother, Matt, came with his children as well. We all shared priceless laughs, hugs, and tears.

Before we departed for Kansas City, we formed a close circle and prayed fervently for his complete healing.

As I said, "Amen," there was scarcely a dry eye in the room. I leaned over to give him one last hug as he whispered something about Inga.

"She reminds me of Melissa. She has her fire."

I whispered back in agreement, "Yes, indeed. I believe Melissa helped hand-pick her."

Inga, Ezekiel, and I drove home in awe of the manifestation of redemption we beheld in that room. Through repeated forgiveness, God performed a mighty work through Melissa's family and ours.

One week later, Melissa's father died. I believe he joined his daughter in Heaven with our children. Before his time on earth ended, he reconciled with God and others.

Complete forgiveness.

Complete redemption.

A personification of no regrets, indeed. I can only wonder if seeing our family gave him a sense of closure and a sort of "permission" to go Home. Only God knows.

Thank God that Inga and I visited him that spring day. If I had followed my weary flesh and not my heart, I would have had regrets to this day. That was our final chance.

Forgive others…today.

Forgive yourself.

Repeatedly.

Let go of the petrified past and delve into God's divine destiny for your life. He has a fantastic future for you – I'm sure of it. That's the kind of God we serve.

Forgive others repeatedly. Start living your life of no regrets today.

Step 7 Action Points

1) Make a no-regrets decision to *Forgive Others Repeatedly*.

2) Make a daily discipline to forgive others' offenses immediately.

3) Pull out the embedded knives of hurt and betrayal.

4) Breathe out the bitterness; breathe in Jesus.

5) Get over every grudge.

6) Let the past be past.

7) Embrace a no regrets future – starting today.

Epilogue

Dream

"So then, anyone who hears these words of mine and obeys them is like a wise man who built his house on rock. The rain poured down, the rivers flooded over, and the wind blew hard against that house. But it did not fall, because it was built on rock." (Matthew 7:24-25 GNT)

"Smile!"

Snap.

The camera shutter clicked and captured a memory – a moment in time.

"Hold it, everyone. Two more!"

My neighbor snapped the pictures on the front lawn of my previous home on Liberty Drive near Kansas City in 2002 – one year before my family died.

On my parents' 50th wedding anniversary, we took a huge family picture with nearly 40 of us all bunched together – parents, children and grandchildren – all huddled beneath my parents' wings. I loved it.

That's my dream.

I just want a big family bursting at the seams with generations nestled beneath our wings. I'm not seeking riches or fame, nor asking God for anything grandiose.

I love family. I love God. I trust Him.

What's your dream? What's the desire of your heart?

Have regrets hampered your hope or clouded your vision?

After reading this book, perhaps the Holy Spirit has surfaced some hidden regrets, grudges, or offenses from your past. Don't feel condemned or guilty. Thank God for revealing them to you.

Now it's time to reconcile them immediately. Let them go. Get right with God and with those individuals at once. You may never get another moment such as this.

Don't let your deepest regret dominate you. Don't let it dampen your dream. Regrets paralyze you in your past. God wants to propel you into a matchless future towards your heart's desires.

I realize it may be difficult to fathom or feel God's love from where you're at right now. If nothing else, believe that it is real and act on it in faith.

God wants to use your story for His glory – if you'll allow Him – if you'll get past your past and press on to the Almighty's divine destiny for you.

Place your past in His hands. Let Him in – to do an incredible work within you and through you.

Your dream may not unfold the way you envisioned. God's ways, His plans, and His thoughts are far above our own. They may not match our plans, but they are always best.

People often ask me how I can have such peace amidst the enduring perpetual pain of missing my heavenly family. My heart is at peace because I have no regrets — with God, with my family, and with myself.

My heart is right with God. I know Him. I've forgiven. I am forgiven. I still worship, trust, and obey God.

I can look back on my family without regrets because I cherished them as best I could while I could. Thirteen years after our first date, I still courted my wife and was faithful to her. I didn't live at the office. I intentionally invested quantity time with our children so we could uncover those rare quality moments that became lasting memories. I didn't live to work; I worked to live.

I allowed my heart to love again and to have children – knowing it could inevitably involve more pain along the way. In spite of everything, I'm still glad I put my heart on the line and didn't shut down for eternity just to avoid more heartache.

Open up! It's worth it – for life, for love, and for God.

Because of my choices and God's boundless grace, He blessed me beyond comprehension with a gracious wife and four more beautiful children already. I cherish my budding family – Inga, Ezekiel, Estellah, Leo, and Lola – beyond description, knowing full well that life is so very fragile.

Inga and I still endure struggles, tears, and difficulties. We aren't perfect. We do our best to practice these principles and extend gobs of grace and buckets of forgiveness with one another.

I believe God has been able to use me and bless us precisely because I've given Him permission to enter in and assume control. I didn't curl up into an immobile wad of pity or regrets.

The morning after my family died, I stood up. The morning after their funeral, I got up. I arose to embrace the future – whatever that meant in God's perplexing plan.

I trust God that much – because I know His character.

I know Him.

I was able to stand up because I still had peace – even amidst the aftermath of that most harrowing tragedy. I had peace of mind with God, others, and myself. That gift of peace came only by knowing God personally through His Son, Jesus Christ.

"I am leaving you with a gift – peace of mind and heart." (John 14:27)

Have you received His gift – His peace? Have you received Him?

Let this day be the first day of your life of no regrets. Keep these simple *7 Steps* close at heart to stay grounded on your path of no regrets. If you slip or stumble, remember that we serve a loving God of second chances.

Rise up and remain on the boundless journey God has for you.

I pray you live a life of no regrets…now and forevermore.

"I have told you all this so that you may have peace in me. Here on earth you will have many trials and sorrows. But take heart, because I have overcome the world."

-Jesus

(John 16:33)

Mighty in the Land Ministry
Teaching Others to Live a Life of No Regrets

In response to ongoing invitations for Robert to tell his family's story, he founded *Mighty in the Land Ministry* to help others **Know God and Live a Life of No Regrets**. Robert still travels the world and freely shares his testimony through music, Scripture, and vivid pictures. (No agent; no fees; pure God). To order his materials or to schedule a life-changing ministry event, contact him by phone at 260.515.5158 or at www.MightyInTheLand.com.

Mighty in the Land FOUNDATION
Dedicated to advance adoption and care for orphans and special-needs children worldwide

Robert has been led to do more than simply tell his story. In 2004, he established the *Mighty in the Land FOUNDATION* orphanage fund with the vision to sponsor at least five orphanages in five regions of the world to honor of his five heavenly family members. To date, seven orphanages have been funded: Russia (2006-Melissa), Rwanda (2008-Makenah), Uganda (2009-Nicholas), Beijing (2010-Alenah), India (2012–Zachary), India (2012-Joy), Uganda (2013-Hope Village of 10 small orphan homes). A portion of this book's proceeds will help care for more orphans. For more information on the *Mighty in the Land FOUNDATION* visit www.MightyInTheLand.com or contact the Foundation directly for various ways you can contribute:

Mighty in the Land Foundation
℅ National Christian Foundation
70 East 91st Street, Suite 101
Indianapolis, IN 46240
317-570-5850